HUD House

by

Nancy Lapidus

with the help of

Arnold Lapidus

hudhousebook@aol.com

ISBN: 1-4033-1060-2 (e-book)
ISBN: 1-4033-1061-0 (Paperback)

Library of Congress Control Number:
2002093211

This book is printed on acid free paper.

Printed in the United States of America
Bloomington, IN

1stBooks - rev. 07/08/02

Table of Contents

The HUD House VIPs

Jake Peterson	Arborist
Henry	Builder
Carpet	
Norman	Carpet dealer
Marion	Carpet planner, salesperson
Rob	Carpet installer
Dennis	Carting company owner
Rich	Crawl space contractor
Vinnie, Marian & their son	Drywallers, painters
Phil	Electrical contractor
Fireplace	
Scoot	Fireplace company owner
Dave	Fireplace salesperson
Marty, Ed & The Gas Guy	Fireplace installers
Cindy	Scoot's assistant
Felicia	Receptionist

The HUD House VIPs

House Inspectors
    Kevin   Chain house inspector
    Tommy   House inspector, carpenter

Maria, Nancy K.,
Audrey, Dale A.,
Kitty, Nicole   HUD employees

Gert   Insurance broker

Charles   Kitchen planner, salesperson

Kenny   Landscaper, handyperson, School bus driver
   Tom   Kenny's assistant

Sean   Landscaper, student, National Guardsman

Lawyer Bill   Poconos area lawyer
  Maisie   Bill's clerk

Katie   Mortgage company representative

Mitch and his
brothers-in-law   Movers

The HUD House VIPs

Plumbing
 Pete   Plumbing contractor
 Charlie   Pete's assistant

Realtors
 Anna   Poconos Realtor
 Sabrina Brown
 Real Estate   Poconos real estate
                 company
 Edna   Chain real estate
                 Realtor
 Loretta
 Lewis   Poconos real estate
                 broker, appraiser
 Phyllis   Realtor,
                 VA specialist

 Joe Thomas   Washington area
                 Realtor

Norm   Roofer, house siding

Buck   Drain & sewer service
                 owner

The HUD House VIPs

Vic   Carpenter, kitchen
                     installer,
                     Home service owner
   Chuck   Vic's assistant

Note: All names have been changed. Except for that change, every word is true.

Introduction

This book is a true, day-to-day journal of ordinary people who obtained a house at a low price through HUD (Housing & Urban Development). With some cash and lots of persistence, we turned an "as-is" wreck into a stylish house, making a modest profit along the way.

People who might be interested in this book are:

- Readers who want a true picture of what it really means to rehabilitate a dilapidated house - what the costs are, how contractors are actually obtained, how to deal with difficult workers, how the weather affects work schedules, to what extent daily life is changed, how to deal with emergencies, and more.
- Families who have received an inheritance but can't afford the payments on an expensive house.
- Workers who have been hired into lucrative jobs which will not last long, but who would like to have a nice house with low payments just in case their jobs are downsized.

- Young people who don't have a big down payment but who expect wage raises they can use to improve their house as time goes on.
- Retirees with some cash, who would like a project and are looking for a nice place to live with low house payments.
- Creative types who require a uniquely fashioned house.

For a long time we had been interested in buying a house, fixing it up and selling it for profit. Superficially, it seemed that you could buy and fix up, but could sell for no more than the purchase price plus the cost of the fix-ups. Doing the math, the holding costs and the commission for selling would likely result in a loss. On the other hand, properties increase in value if they are converted to their best and highest use. If you bought a substandard house and sold it as a standard house it might increase in value above the purchase price plus improvements. Furthermore, if the house were stylish, it might command a premium for style. However, houses in our area in New Jersey were too high-priced and hardly ever sold at foreclosure or at bargain prices unless they were too far gone.

The Pocono Mountains area in Pennsylvania is just 75 miles from the George Washington Bridge in New York. You get there by Route 80, an easy, straight highway, making it a convenient vacation destination and a possible commute to and from the city. In fact, the population has grown 40% in the last ten years. The low crime rate appeals to New York parents, who see it as a safe place where their children can get a decent public education.

Housing costs are low compared to New York City. A small but livable house can be had for $50,000 and up. Occasionally, there are homes priced in the $200,000's or $300,000's, but in New York suburbs such higher prices are typical.

While Aventis Pasteur has a large presence here, high-paying technology jobs are not that easy to find. The area was recently known for coal mining and has skipped the manufacturing stage. Residents who work in the area often have two and three jobs to enable them to support their families. The main industries are construction and tourism.

Recently, retirees from the urban areas have found the Poconos attractive. Many recreational facilities such as uncrowded tennis courts, golf courses, communities with pools, lakes and beaches, and ski resorts are accessible, and are close to the towns where their children and grandchildren live.

The Poconos are a recreation asset that has been under-utilized in the Northeast in favor of areas with cachet such as the Hamptons, Fire Island and Cape Cod.

We chose the Poconos for a pilot project because it was a vacation neighborhood familiar to us, and we had a sense of what the values were. If a property came up that was undervalued we might be able to buy it. Other readers might choose a different area for other reasons, but being familiar with the neighborhood is important. We picked a house in the Poconos that needed a lot of work, but which had an outstanding feature: lots of glass doors and windows looking out onto the forest. It cost $44,000. We bought it with $15,000 down. Repairs, furnishings and utilities came to $9,500. After paying sales commission, we realized a profit of

$8,500 not counting transportation and effort. We celebrated with a steak dinner at the Smith & Wollensky Steak House in New York.

We decided to go ahead with another house. We first bid on a FannieMae foreclosure. Using a rudimentary spreadsheet analysis, we arrived at what we thought was a fair and objective bid based on our estimate of the costs to make it livable: adding in hidden costs charged by the development, such as $600 per year for water; closing costs; sales commission and a reasonable profit. FannieMae ignored our bid.

We next tried to buy a bank foreclosure. We had it inspected before making our offer because the damage seemed extensive and we wanted to make a repair estimate beforehand. The damage was even greater than we thought. We offered $43,000 to their asking price of $63,000, accompanied by an explanation. The bank turned us down and made a counteroffer only a few thousand below their asking price. Then the previously mentioned FannieMae agency suggested it might take our offer on the first house we bid on if we applied again.

By this time we were certain we didn't want it. Among other negatives, the association required repairs to be made by contractors selected from their exclusive list.

We decided to try HUD as a primary agent, rather than going through the usual Realtor channel. The HUD houses were appearing on the Internet for bids the same day they became available, so we would not be getting leftovers. All the other bidders would be equally looking for bargains - nobody wants to overpay. We wouldn't be subject to any salesmanship. The appraised value by a government appraisal is based on the value of the house, while the price of a bank foreclosure might depend more on the amount of debt than on the actual worth of the house. It was with this background that we decided to search the Internet for a HUD foreclosure.

February to June: Discovery to Closing

2/28

Signing onto the Internet, Arnie locates two HUD houses in the Pennsylvania Poconos. The houses are in developments we recognize. They seem to be worth a look.

3/2

We click on the map shown on the Internet listing and get driving directions to the houses. We're surprised to find the first house appealing, but garage door panels are dented in, the deck railing over the garage is warped and broken, a piece of the siding is hanging down from the upper deck. The front door opens directly into a huge great room with lots of windows, and there is a fireplace containing a broken wood stove insert. The large kitchen lacks either range or dishwasher.

A nice stairway with a view of the great room from a loft-type landing could be charming. One bedroom is very large, with a small, high window letting in extra light, and sliding glass doors leading out to a roof deck. Two smaller bedrooms are functional.

The directions to the second house are incomprehensible, so we decide to ignore it.

We want to bid on the house we have just seen. The bid must be submitted through a broker. I call HUD and ask if they have a broker who can do it. They suggest the nearest broker, Sabrina Brown Agency, in the same town as the house. I ask if large chain brokers are allowed to do it. They are.

3/4

I call Edna, a Realtor who has done good work for us in the past. She has never bid on a HUD house via the Internet, but would like to try. I agree to coach her through the steps to making a bid, but although she knows her real estate computer system, she doesn't know how to use the mouse on the Internet. It's too frustrating for her. She is uncomfortable about giving her social security number, required for presenting the phone bid. She suggests I call the Sabrina Brown company.

The Sabrina Brown agent is enthusiastic. I tell her my bid,

and she says she will submit it right away. I should hear from her tonight or Saturday morning.

3/5

Saturday morning passes. I leave voice mail. No reply.

3/6

I call her office on Sunday. After screening my call they tell me she's on another line and will call me back. An hour goes by. I call again. They tell me she has left the office. It's now clear she can't or won't submit our bid. I leave word that I am canceling my request to her and will find another broker who would like to help me.

I call Anna, a young agent I have dealt with in the past, a Columbia University graduate student who is computer savvy. She agrees to act and submits our bid. The only way we will know if our bid is accepted is by inference. If our bid price and the broker's name appear on screen as an accepted bid, it means we have it.

3/9

The asking price when we first saw the listing was $44,000, but it has now been reduced to $40,800. Sometime earlier on the Internet we noticed that the FannieMae administration was accepting bids at about 9% less its asking price, so we computed 9% of $40,800, deducted that from the asking price, rounded down, and came up with a bid of $37,000. After 24 hours of checking on the Internet, no sale is announced. Anna says this means that our bid was rejected. No reason need be given for a rejected bid. We up our bid to $40,000 and resubmit it.

3/10

This time it is accepted, but today it shows a bid of $25,000 was submitted by another broker in this area just three hours before ours.

3/11-3/30

A mortgage company is contacted, and a pre-qualification form is requested. Their agent cooperates and faxes one within a few hours. This is typical. Anna mails contract forms and instructions to us by overnight mail. I return these to her by express mail, together with the pre-qualification form and a $500 money order as deposit (usually 1% of the bid is enough).

We decide to proceed with a home inspection, but we need to get electricity and water turned on. I arrange for all of these. We apply formally to HUD to request permission to inspect, enclosing a $50 money order to pay HUD for turning on the electricity and water and then turning it off when the inspection is over. (HUD doesn't know if we will actually go through with the sale and does not wish to incur any extra utility expense. Additionally, in northeast winters the water must be shut off so that plumbing pipes do not freeze.) I put the electricity and water accounts in my name and plan to leave them on. We will re-winterize the plumbing after the inspection is over.

Fortunately, the inspection service representative was very careful and asked me to check that the utilities were actually on. In fact, the water company never told me somebody had to be present, and they have done nothing, since "nobody was home" when they arrived. Not thoughtful, since this is a vacation area and many people are weekenders. At the same time, HUD returns our money order and refuses permission to inspect until we receive the contract actually signed by them.

We arrange with Anna to take this opportunity to look at the house closely, since she has already scheduled this appointment. We find that there is at least a foot of water in the basement. The main lever controlling the circuit box won't budge, even though the power is on, and several of the circuits are unconnected, trailing wires hanging from the leads. The rest of the house is as we first saw it: badly stained and smelly carpets; bad paint, most of it bubblegum pink. A large animal cage containing unknown material distributed in straw stands in one corner of the garage.

We engage an electrician to get the main lever moving, which he does. He checks out the system and gives us an estimate of the job to be done. He doesn't want to leave the sump pump unattended, so he shuts down the main lever when he goes.

3/31

Anna calls about the signed contract, which we think we should have received by now. The HUD representative tells her we have to wait for their time frame.

We send e-mail to the HUD representative inquiring what a reasonable time should be for receiving the signed contract. (We never received a reply.)

4/4

I phone the "broad sales representative," whose role is usually assumed by the selling broker in private transactions. Angela tells me the contract was signed on 3/17, and we should be getting it any day now.

4/8

Still no reply. Anna calls and tries to get a copy of the signed contract. She is refused. However, they will have the local volunteer fire department pump out the basement.

4/11

I call the legal department of my union, the United Federation of Teachers, because I am concerned that I have not yet received a signed contract, but the closing date is less than three weeks away. The lawyer advises that I proceed with the mortgage application and try to get the inspection, because the 4/30 closing date is hard to extend.

4/14

Arnie calls Anna. He tells her he thinks this delay is beyond reason and suggests her manager press HUD to act. They call. They get Maria. She obtains permission to fax us a copy of the signed contract. She explains that since HUD is new in this area they haven't decided on a title company. Anna resubmits the request for inspection. They will give a 30-day extension of the closing date to 5/30.

4/15,16,17

We don't receive the promised copy of the signed contract. We begin to think HUD actually doesn't have clear title. We delay submitting our mortgage application in spite of the union lawyer's advice because the application fee is $375, an amount we wouldn't like to lose if the sale doesn't occur.

We receive and accept a formal offer on our New Jersey house. The closing date is set for June 30.

We ask the attorney for our New Jersey house transaction for a use and occupancy clause. Such a clause entitles us to lease the house back from the buyer for 30 days in the event we need more time to move.

We receive a faxed copy of the first page of the signed HUD contract!

Anna informs us that she has re-sent our returned inspection request, accompanied by a $50 money order, to the broad listing broker for HUD.

We arrange to have a key to the house and go there with a pump, just in case. There is still a foot of water in the crawl space. We have enough working electricity to start pumping, but after six hours the water level has gone down only an inch. We buy a second pump, but it's time to return the key to the broker.

4/20

Arnie makes calls: To Maria (phone is busy, busy, busy), to Nancy K. (will be in on Monday), then to Audrey, who gives him the name and phone of Dale A. She is the person who knows. She explains they are in the process of having closing companies apportioned to handle the closing and expects to proceed quickly, probably closing in May.

Anna calls, says Kitty can give permission to pump out the water. Anna thinks we will close in May. "It will be closed in May," she says.

4/21

Anna says that when Maria received the renewed inspection request she forwarded it to Nicole. As it happens, Nicole was the wrong person to receive it. Nicole will FedEx it to the correct person, who should receive it on Monday. Meanwhile, our broker can't find the key we returned and has to trace it.

4/25

Anna tells me the inspection request has not been received. Kitty is trying to find it. Yes, we may pump out the water. The Fire Department never returned Kitty's call of 4/8. This is an example of someone making a commitment for someone else. It rarely works.

4/26

Anna calls. The person to whom Maria sent the inspection requests has resigned. The request is now sitting on that person's desk. It will be sent to the correct person. I call Maria to find out to whom it is being sent. She is not in. I leave a message. No return call.

I call the teachers' union legal service. They agree we need legal representation and will try to get us a lawyer in our area. However, the lawyers they have are actually quite distant, so we decide to choose one on our own.

From the Yellow Pages, Arnie finds a lawyer local to the house who deals in real estate, speaks to him and decides to retain him. The lawyer also knows Anna. I call Anna to see if there is any news. Permission for inspection is imminent - she will keep after them. She gets permission for inspection.

Do You Need a Lawyer For Real Estate Deals?

In some areas it is customary to hire a lawyer. In others a title insurance company handles the transaction. We have done this both ways. Where we lived in New Jersey it was customary to hire a lawyer. In one attempted transaction the lawyer was deceived by a ploy of the prospective buyers to take thousands of dollars off the price agreed upon. Needless to say, we could not consent to this, and the deal fell through. Another lawyer from the same area was very experienced, and the closing went like a dream. We had one transaction with a title company that made many errors totaling about $1,500 and who forgot to ask for the home insurance check. On the other hand, I handled a transaction for my brother in Florida where the title company went through all the difficulties of a touchy condo board and handled them well, all by phone. In this HUD case, 20 minutes after calling our lawyer we got permission to inspect. Perhaps he pointed out that it was not legal for them to have a contract without a closing date. It also turned out he was the president of the county bar association, so was probably very smooth.

We call Pete the Plumber to request he pump the water out at our cost, locate the main water valve in case it leaks when the water is turned on and give the plumbing a once-over.

4/30

I leave a message on Anna's voice mail informing her we have hired a lawyer and identifying him.

5/1

I call the mortgage company's agent to make sure all is going smoothly.

5/2

No reply. Call again. Katie the Mortgage Lady tells me all is going well. The bank appraiser will go out next week. They expect to be able to close 5/25. Will check whether they need a water test.

Arnie calls our lawyer to check on the progress. He tells us we have a closing company and a person to contact. June 8 is the closing. We all agree to a time of 2:00 p.m. at the lawyer's office. I inform Anna.

5/3

Pete the Plumber calls. It will cost $200 to pump out the water, but $288 to install a proper sump pump and keep it pumping out any water that comes in again from rain. We agree. He leaves us his best heavy-duty $50 extension cord, to be returned. He advises us not to have water turned on, as some broken pipes will spew sprays of water even though the main valve is closed. He will return the key to our broker.

5/4

The inspection is re-arranged for 5/11 at 1:30. We inform the inspector that water won't be turned on. Also, boots may be needed. I call Anna, inform her that the closing won't be in some distant town as she had thought. She is delighted, and relaxes.

5/9

Receive notification from the bank requesting this year's tax return and the latest statement from my investment companies. We don't think we should have to tell all - just enough to qualify for the loan. We will seriously consider paying cash next time.

A truth-in-lending statement dated 4/26 but postmarked 5/6 is received from the bank. We are supposed to agree to the rate of 8.9%. (When we began this transaction the quoted rate was 8.75%).

5/11

The inspection is handled by Anna and Arnie. When they arrive there is a foot of water in the crawl space because the sump pump was not connected to the hose. Our Pete the Plumber did this. The water valve is submerged, and the crawl space can't be inspected. The inspection report is long, worse than we thought. Shortcuts were allegedly taken in construction.

5/12

We feel the worst problem is the four-inch wall thickness that doesn't allow proper insulation. How will we keep warm this winter? We decide to go to the bobvila.com site on the Internet and use the Ask Bob feature to see if there is some ordinary solution. If it can be solved we will go ahead. If not, we might try to escape. However, we will continue with the inspection.

Results of the Inspection

1. Insulation and heating are badly wanting. The kitchen isn't heated at all.
2. The garage roof is leaking (we thought that).
3. The electrical system is inadequate (we knew that).
4. The fireplace has no damper - a fireplace expert has to look further.
5. There is no stove, there are holes in the drywall, the fridge is mold-encrusted, cabinets are missing, the floor covering is damaged.
6. The bathrooms have cracked tiles, one cracked toilet, broken drywall.
7. Broken front door, garage door needs replacing (we knew that).
8. Carpet on the roof deck keeps it damp, moss is growing.
9. There are weak rails on the roof deck.
10. Bulbs are missing in recessed lighting - do the fixtures work?
11. Septic vent caps missing, probably needs septic tank pumped.

And so on…

5/13

Second thoughts:

1. We have to move.
2. We might use this as a three-season house.
3. We might fix one wall at a time.
4. We might fix it ourselves.

To continue with the inspection we need to get the septic pump working and the basement pumped out. Pete is called. The sump pump may be clogged. He will get it going for a $45 charge. The appraiser may have the key yet. He will check.

I call Anna. She is reluctant to say it's OK to get the septic pump going. We are to call the lawyer.

5/15

Lawyer Bill thought Anna wasn't going to be involved. I inform him there are things she is required to do by HUD, such as to be present at the inspection. He will get permission for us to hook up the septic pump so we can complete the inspection, and inform Anna we can do this.

Anna has received a message from him, calls us first. Arnie informs her. Asks if she has ever heard of an entire septic system needing replacement. In fact, she had bought a FannieMae foreclosure which needed replacement, but they paid for it.

5/16

Our lawyer calls, says HUD won't pay for it. I clarify that we will pay, just were told we couldn't do it without permission. He can't understand why we want an inspection if we are buying "as is." I explain we need to know what's wrong so we can arrange for workers to do the job.

Today it becomes apparent why living two hours away is a problem. If we were closer, we could check if the sump pump has actually cleared out the basement and arrange for the water company to turn the water on.

We would like the septic tested, but may ask our plumber to do that if it's not possible with the home inspector.

I call Phil the Electrician. He is in a cherry-picker, prefers to discuss an appointment when he's on the ground. We make a telephone appointment. We arrange to have the septic pump electricity connected by the end of the week.

5/17

Anna calls. Says Pete didn't return the key. I clarify. Apparently, her office gave Pete the key returned by the appraiser, never opening the key envelope she left for him. The unopened envelope with the key in it is still at the desk. She will call Phil to let him know the key is available.

5/18

Phil calls. The septic pump is connected and working. He has been in the crawl space and noted additional lines that need work. Also took a look at the septic system. Three of the six vents have problems, one uncapped (we knew) and two are cracked and will need replacement. We are merely relieved he didn't sink into the mud of the crawl space.

5/19

I call the water company to get water turned on. I make an appointment for the afternoon so I have time to get there.

We receive a lock-in agreement from the mortgage company at a 9.23% rate. Didn't I call when it was 8.593 to lock it in? Is this truth in lending?

5/20

We call the inspection company for a new inspection. They tell me they are booked until 5/30. We call Tommy the Carpenter, who has done good work for us over the years. He does inspections. We had not called him before this because we thought this jewel of a house might be coveted by others. The inspection company calls, can have another man drop by on his way, would charge $250 for the basement inspection and about the same for a septic inspection. I don't think so. Tommy tells me he can do it, will know early Thursday the day and time. I am to call him at 7:30 a.m. I inform Anna of both appointments.

The Bob Vila staff replies to my e-mail query. They think a re-wrap of the house could be done or the ceiling dropped and insulation inserted, but either method would be very pricey.

5/22

I call the real estate agent's office to check that there is a key ready for tomorrow. Anna isn't in. The receptionist knows nothing. He transfers my call to Anna's voice mail. Anna calls me back and verifies that a key is actually taped to the front desk.

5/23

I call the water company to verify my appointment with them for this afternoon. All is go. I drive to the house with a book, a magazine, a chair, a pad with telephone numbers and a jar. I check my cell phone. I don't think about a flashlight to check that the basement is still dry. I hadn't been to the house in a while. It has nice bones in spite of all its faults. I check on some things mentioned in the inspection report. Cracks in the bathroom tiles are not that evident or numerous. Two tiles were poorly placed at the edge to begin with. I think I can fix them. The cause of the sagging section of the living room floor seems clear. It ought to be a bad joist in the crawl space. The kitchen cabinets were not hung quite level. A corner cabinet that would adjoin the stove makes no sense. There is no door on one half. The other half is a squeeze to get into. The drawer opens into a space reserved for the oven. The wall cabinet above it goes through to the end of the wall, but can't be used because it is in the corner. Who planned this? I settle into my chair to read. Nobody shows by three o'clock. I turn on my cell phone, and the Ericsson AT&T phone, for which we especially asked for Pocono service, reads "No Service." I wait until 4:50. I leave a note in the door and drive to a phone. I speak to Marcy. Quoting their telephone motto, "Customer service is our first priority," I tell her that I verified my appointment but nobody showed up. She reports that the appointment was canceled. It seems that someone with a similar name canceled, so they took me off the list. Marcy will radio out. I will go to the house. If nobody comes within an hour I will call back. After a half hour a cheery young man arrives. They have called him at home. He turns on the water, asks if water is on inside. Although Pete turned the water off the meter is running. I had thought

I would borrow a flashlight to look into the crawl space, but here's a good opportunity. He climbs down and turns off the valve. Good guy. He goes back to check the meter. Who turned the water valve on? Maybe whoever peed in the toilet and, then, poor person, found there was no water. The water man refuses a tip. I will do a good deed for someone in his name.

I return to Anna's office with the key. Her office is closed for the day. But we have water. I am deliriously happy.

Persistence conquers.—J.P.Morgan. When dealing with bureaucracies, patience is the card to play. —Norman Mailer in Harlot's Ghost

5/25

I call Tommy the Carpenter at 7:30. No answer. We are planning what else to do, when he calls. He had to walk his dog. He will charge $50 and get a plumber to inspect the septic system. If he can't get a plumber we will ask Pete to do it. We're set for Saturday at noon. Anna is informed.

At this point we have decided that we will take the house in any circumstance. Arnie figures that the permits, the septic, the existing structures and the land are worth about $37,000.

Land	12,000
Perk test compliance	4,000
House	21,000
Total	37,000

Because it's worth at least $37,000 and we're paying $40,000, the most we'd be losing is $3,000. But since HUD appraised it as $44,000 originally, we're probably getting our money's worth.

5/27

We meet Tommy at the house. Arnie finds a small puddle, but mostly it is dry in the crawl space. Tommy finds the sump pump tipped over and constantly running, quite hot, and rights it. The foundation is okay. Some joists are wet, don't need replacement, merely to run a fan on a humidistat, as Arnie had suggested. He sees definite leaks from the roof, in the form of water mark streaks across the ceiling. Ice guard installation in strategic spots should take care of it - remove shingles, install guards and replace shingles. Confirms we need a rubber roof on the dust porch (roof deck), new railings. Windows show signs of leaking, need caulking. Ten-mil plastic is to be laid on the crawl space floor and pulled up over the lip and secured. Elbow pipe at the main water line should be replaced, as water flows from valve onto the ground when inside water is opened.

Anna arrives, asks how things are going. She seems actually disappointed that we are going ahead. Tommy picks up on this, says about me, "She doesn't give up." We all laugh.

It looks as though the septic inspection is too difficult to arrange. We don't actually say this, but Anna urges a septic inspection, citing an instance where customers didn't inspect anything although she told them they ought to, then sued her company for misrepresentation when they found a failed septic. Arnie asks again if they ever heard of the entire septic needing replacement. Tommy said he hadn't, just repairs. All in all, this was much better than we expected. We feared foundation repairs and rotted joists. Arnie thinks $50 is too little for Tommy's fee, pays more.

We ride over to a house across the road - a bank foreclosure on which we had bid $47,000 in January from a $69,000 asking price, because of anticipated extreme foundation work, wall rebuilding and landscape regrading, among many other things. The bank did not accept our bid or submit what we considered a reasonable counteroffer. Arnie didn't really like its location within its development, and our agent was not strong in the negotiation, so we dropped it. When we returned to look at it we found it was occupied. The front steps had been fixed and the fallen tree in the yard had been sawn into smaller pieces. There were clothes hanging in the yard. But Arnie was right about the location - it looked rather seedy, and I was glad we were getting the HUD house.

5/29
   Memorial Day - take a holiday.

5/30
   Call Pete. Ask him to:

1. Fix elbow joint where water is pouring out from main line when water valve to house is turned on.
2. Fix main floor toilet, which may be stuffed.
3. Fix leak under sink.
4. Perform at least an eyeball inspection of the septic tank system.

I call Gert the Insurance Lady. Katie the Mortgage Lady has not gotten back to her to send her a required clause for the insurance policy. I read Gert the required clause so she can include it in her policy.

6/1
I call Pete. He says Anna is now only a seller's agent for her broker, and he has just gotten the key late this afternoon.

6/2
Pete calls. He fixed the toilet and the elbow; the leak under the sink is only an unattached trap. The charge is $288 (this seems to be a favorite price). He thinks the septic is okay, but would feel better if a person who can certify

it looks at it. We decide we are so close to closing we will call him afterwards.

I call Lawyer Bill to check that the closing will take place. He will double check to verify that date of June 8. I tell him insurance is in the works. He says I will next hear from his office about the amount of the certified check to be brought to the closing.

6/3

I call Katie the Mortgage Lady to make sure she has gotten in touch with the insurance company. All is well.

6/4

We receive an application for signature and receipt for $213 insurance. This goes into my envelope for HUD immediately. We express mail a check to Gert. If we didn't know each other I would express mail the check and enclose an express mail envelope addressed to the lawyer for sending the receipt, then phone the lawyer to tell him to expect it.

I call Anna, telling her that I have heard she isn't my representative anymore and to call me about a transition. (Do we need to verify that we accept the rules and regulations of the association?)

6/5

Anna doesn't call back. I call her broker, who explains Anna will see us through. Apparently, she is going to marry in October. She expects her master's degree in social work, too, and is leaving real estate.

Arnie calls the septic man, still thinking it is better to have it looked at. He is too busy. No later date is set.

6/6

I call Lawyer Bill to tell him I need a figure for a bank check. Maisie is working on it now. I am also concerned that we have not yet produced the required statement that we agree to abide by the rules and regulations of the homeowners' association. He tells me the broker usually takes care of that. I tell him I have a copy of the regulations and spoke with them, and will try to get to my broker. I call Anna and get her in. In fact, she's on the phone with the attorney. We all decide we can go ahead without the actual form. Maisie comes up with a figure of $18,884.08, our down payment and closing fees.

6/7

I get a bank check. When I return I find a new, different figure has come in. Arnie goes to the bank and obtains an additional $271 bank check to cover the difference. By the time he returns Maisie has called to say they had not included the $500 deposit at my broker's escrow and will have to give me a refund check.

Can Poor-to-Ordinary People Buy a HUD Home?

1. *This was a very costly process till now.*

   A) *We had to retain a lawyer, not customary in this area, where a only a title insurance company is usually obtained. ($300)*

   B) *In order to do the inspections we had to pay for extensive repairs in advance - $576 for plumbing - pumping out the basement, repairing pipes so water could be run; electrical repairs so that the sump pump and septic pumps could run*

($66), all of which would be lost if we decided against the house.

C) *Extensive phone bills to Pennsylvania to plumbers, electricians, water, electric and phone companies, bank, garbage removal, inspectors and real estate agents were incurred. Whole mornings were spent on the phone making arrangements.*

D) *Three inspections would have run $250 each.*

2. *It will be a costly process to reclaim this house. At this point we estimate $20,000 for plumbing, electricity, roofing, painting, carpeting, fumigating and exterminating. Another 20% overrun is possible, or $4,000 for the unexpected = $24,000.*

3. *If a home improvement loan is obtained the house costs $64,000 plus closing costs.*

4. *The complexity of the procedure was so great that two Realtors turned it down at the outset. Buyers would have to know which Realtor could help them. Why would a layman know that? In some areas of the country some real estate agents advertise their specialty, but in this area they do not.*

5.   Before we had a lawyer neither we nor our Realtor could penetrate the organization of the broad agent. We didn't know who was in charge of the various aspects of the sale.   We couldn't obtain titles of the people we spoke to or   determine   their responsibilities. They themselves didn't seem to understand local organization, either.   Example: For some reason the broad agent expected the volunteer fire department to pump out the basement that was flooded because HUD had shut off the electricity that ran the sump pump.

An article in the Washington Times Home Guide explained that the Veterans Administration pays so little to the broad agent that they are not motivated to cooperate. Here, the broad agent was getting $400. However, they seemed to be doing extra work by avoiding the work. Effort was required to overcome this inertia.

6/8

We pack up all our documents and bank checks. We start out early to take a dry run to the lawyer's office, then pick up some paint at Sears on our way to the house. We think we should look in just before closing and make sure no disaster has occurred. This walk-through is often done with the Realtor, and one is entitled to it, but since we have the key it's not necessary to bother Anna. We remove the various For Sale signs.

Lawyer Bill is super. All is well organized. We start. Soon Anna arrives; then Katie for the bank, with a box of chocolates for us. The lawyer explains each form as we sign it. The documents are passed around to each person who has to sign. Chatting reveals factors that played a part in the attitudes and delays. Apparently, the former broad selling agent had gone bankrupt, and the new one had just been appointed. They, in turn, had not yet selected a closing company and so would not give a closing date. About 100 other people and we were caught in this morass. Our Realtor was in litigation with a client who found septic tank troubles and was claiming they had never been advised to inspect. Anna thought we couldn't pass appraisal if there was no stove and informed us. In fact, she said it again at the closing in Katie's presence. We all laughed, and the lawyer told her she shouldn't be saying that now.

I presented Anna with a dramatic-looking cyclamen plant for seeing us through this mess; Katie gave us her box of chocolates; we got a deed; Anna, HUD's closer and the lawyer all got checks.

WE OWN THE HOUSE!

June to July: Moving

6/8

The first thing to do was to change the locks. One job goes well, but the second lock doesn't fit. Incidentally, we later learn we could have paid about $13 in Home Depot for what we paid $24 locally.

We bring in painting materials from the car in preparation for painting two rooms before moving in: we think it would be more efficient if the room for Arnie's office/library was painted before all the books and computer supplies are moved in. We also think it would be good to paint one small bedroom for livability.

6/15

We arrange to have two-foot high grass mown. Cost: $100.

6/23

We bring a coffee maker and sleeping bags the night before meeting Phil the Electrician. We must buy a mattress and a box spring.

Phil the Electrician and his assistant arrive. As mentioned

earlier, Phil had given us an evaluation. He thought that the wiring in the house was okay but needed checking, and the main circuits had to be connected to the wiring. There were also some loose wires in the basement, which he thought should be reinstalled and brought up to safe standards. His assistant labels the circuit breakers in addition to helping with simple tasks like moving bulbs and shouting out whether a light is on or off. The very high ceilings have recessed lights, which aren't working. We thought it might turn out to be expensive to get them on, but Phil finds that an amateur had purposely disconnected five of the lights and had put the sixth on an upstairs switch. He brings in a very high ladder to reach the lights in the vaulted ceiling and get all the recessed lights working perfectly. His helper found out that covers for the lights are available at Home Depot for about $4, each of which might otherwise have cost $20 each. Arnie thinks we should get them at Home Depot instead of painting the ones that are already there, and Phil gives him a long list of about $150 worth of electrical supplies to buy, as long as he would already be there. The Home Depot salesman is pretty knowledgeable but not perfect, and Arnie has to point out that the size he recommended for high hat fixtures would not fit.

The circuit breakers are modules that fit into the circuit breaker box. They cost $5-10 each, depending on technical features such as single pole or double pole. Arnie and Phil originally thought that there was a partial installation of a new circuit box. Arnie now thinks that someone merely removed the modules to obtain a salvage value of about $30-40, not caring about the consequences. The electrical hookup for the dishwasher is dangerous and needs upgrading. There is a switch placed half in the wainscoting and half on the wall, necessitating an interruption in the wainscot edging, which looks inappropriate. We want to raise the switch about two inches above the wainscoting. Phil says he could do it, but he would not recommend it because it would be a harder installation than doing the original, which was in the wrong place. This is good advice: the correction would be disproportional to the cost, about $200.

We thought that the garage door opener was a lost cause and were budgeting about $500 for it, but Phil gets it running, and we are all delighted and play with it for a while. This leaves just a couple of electrical odds and ends to be done. Outdoor outlets and many garage outlets now work. We are also delighted that the rear door halogen lights work.

In summary, the cost was about $500, and many upscale features such as the garage door opener, overhead fans, halogen light and recessed lighting, in addition to the regular lighting and the many outlets in the house, are now operable.

Some outdoor lighting is still to be done. This job has gone very well. We actually expected much more trouble and much more expense.

I paint the office.

Can You Really Phone a Mattress?

A mattress-by-phone company has informed us that deliveries are made on Tuesdays and Fridays in our area, and that if we call the day before *for a Tuesday delivery it is assured. We call on Monday evening and can't get through. We are on a recorded commercial that doesn't end. We sleep on the floor in sleeping bags. The pet odor is acrid, and we have a restless night. We decide to call the company very early Tuesday morning. After initial difficulty, Pamela promises Arnie an $800 mattress, box spring and frame, with free delivery and setup and an excellent buy on a mattress pad. It is to arrive between 1 and 6 p.m.*

At 3:30 p.m. we decide to check on the mattress delivery. We are told it won't be coming until Friday. The whole system is a mess - various departments check, some of which have no record of the sale. Pamela is said to have gone home. There is no hope of getting it today. We cancel the order, also with difficulty. We decide to start home to New Jersey, stopping at mattress stores on the way. The first one has closed at 5 p.m. We stop at Sears, but this branch has no furniture. At the mall information booth we are directed to a franchise mattress store. We think their prices are way out of proportion.

> *We head home, sans mattress.*
> *To be fair, we had dealt with this company twice in the past and found them to be quite efficient and low-priced.*

7/5

We decide we are close enough to moving to forego the mattress. We can use our sleeper couch and wait for a department store sale.

7/6

The mail system in this housing development is that there is a bank of mailboxes, and you go to your assigned box in that bank to pick up the mail. We need a post office box, as the mailboxes provided are too small for the amount of mail we receive.

We want to carpet two rooms - the office/library and one small bedroom. We decide against bargain carpet because we know a reasonable, honest place that did a good job of laying carpet in a previous house. A sloppy or dishonest job can ruin the whole thing, as we have previously experienced. The carpet people remember us, and cooperate to get the job done on time. After I apologize for the pet odors on the old carpet, they offer to disinfect the basic floor, a service sorely needed.

On the way to the post office we see a sign, 'MATTRESSES $99 EACH PIECE, ANY SIZE." We double back and try them out. Of course, the more expensive ones are better, and we opt for a set of those if they can deliver it today in two hours, when we return from the post office. It's still cheaper than mattress-by-phone or the chain store, and they deliver it within three hours. The owner can't get the regular delivery person on the phone, so he brings it himself. Arnie has to help him, and his shoulder hurts now.

I paint the small bedroom. My error: It didn't really register on me that the room was pink. I'm using lots of paint to cover it, and I'm short about a quart. A professional painter once told me that pink and green are the hardest colors to cover. Arnie goes to Sears to get another can. This takes him almost two hours, a bad mistake on my part, but the extra won't go to waste - the kitchen and bathroom are pink also.

Arnie brings in his computers, puts them in a room and locks the door.

7/12

Norman the Carpet Man calls. He's scared because the actual dimensions are a bit more than estimated, but I say, "Well, what can we do? Go ahead with it." It wasn't really that much different, and he's relieved I didn't have a fit.

7/14

"Camping in" without a range and a fridge hasn't really been efficient. The nearest convenience store is about two miles away. The nearest restaurant is 2-1/2 miles away, and we have been spending a lot of time just eating. We shop for a range and fridge in the area and find our best deal at Home Depot. Arnie wants one with many extras such as ice maker and water filter. We had lived with a very minimal fridge in New Jersey for many years because there was only one that fit in the spot for it, and it had nothing extra. I think he's right. We go for a fancy side-by-side with extra features. It is absolutely gorgeous. However, I skimp by ordering an electric range with an ordinary surface, not a smooth top, because I also think that the smooth top will get scratched and look bad over time. I don't want the tension of being careful every time I cook.

Nice job on the carpets. Someone has tried the locked upstairs bedroom door and pulled the jamb apart.

7/17

The move from a seven-room house, including two loads to a storage facility costs under $2,000. Arnie had gotten an estimate for moving from the Internet for $4,000-8,000. He thought this was out of proportion. From a neighborhood New Jersey newspaper, he found the number of a mover. He thought he would see how the mover did by moving a van load of boxes into the storage facility. Then he tried him with a second load. The mover came from nearby Westchester. Arnie had found that many Westchester businessman were honest and competent. Satisfied, he discussed the move to Pennsylvania with them and struck a deal.

Moving day. The movers are efficient and very congenial. They must know how to handle jittery relocaters. They will follow us to the new house. Of course, we have provided written directions just in case, but it's a tense trip.

At the house we have to provide instant directives about where things go. Again, the movers are very efficient. Toward the end of the move you can see how tired they are, but they keep up a happy face. They congratulate us on our swell packing job. We had put nearly all our things in boxes, sealed and labeled. Mitch the Mover offers to do the roof job. He thinks it needs it because when we arrived there were some puddles on the garage floor where the roof had apparently leaked. Arnie thinks he will have a high price for the roof because he comes from a much more prosperous area, and there would be four hours travel time each day to do it. But it would be done right. Mitch points out that it gives us another option.

The entire move plus two hours traveling is done between 8:30 a.m. and 1:30 p.m. Total damage: one broken wine glass and a missing knob from a night table.

July: A rung up from camping

7/18

Time to get down to basics. We buy a new faucet for the leaky upstairs sink, porcelain fixer and a wire brush to repair the cracked toilet fixture, a cheap new toilet seat, and replacement lampshades for the ceiling fan. Lots of cleaning is required before shelving and distributing dishes and food into the cabinets. I spray the driveway with weed killers - there are too many to remove by hand. I call the garbage removal company, but get no answer. We install house numbers.

The carpets smell so bad they interfere with sleep, even in the new bed. We decide to carpet the master bedroom right away. I go to the carpet store to pay the bill for the two rooms they already did, retrieve the key and select new carpet.

7/19

There are holes in the window screens. We could take them to a local hardware store, but decide to develop a new skill. We buy hardware cloth, spline and a splining tool, then discover the screens have a self-system of metal splines that snap in and pry out. It takes a few hours for Arnie to do three screens, but we didn't have to wait, and we didn't have to travel to retrieve them.

Shower curtains are now a priority because there are cartons in the bathrooms that can get wet. I retrieve some while Arnie is repairing screens.

7/20

Carpet installers arrive at 7:30 a.m. and take measurements. I call another garbage service after trying to reach the first one for days. They offer to take three trash bags once a week, with additional bags and special items at extra cost. I have to think about it. An hour later the first service returns my call. They have a better deal, taking three cans a week with as much as you want to put in them, tied or bagged newspapers free, recycling in a community can. This is a better deal. We agree to start tomorrow.

The range and refrigerator arrive and are installed. Now we see what bad planning can do. The electric range has to be located where its special outlet is located. Therefore, the drawers and door of the base cabinet at right angles to it are not functional. The cabinet drawer will open only if the oven door is open. We decide to keep light bulbs in that drawer. Half the base cabinet is dead space. I can keep a few seldom-used items in the other half, if I open the door part way.

7/21

Pete the Plumber arrives in the afternoon, installs the new kitchen faucet and the fridge ice maker. The ice maker kit was sold separately to be installed by the owner, but it is actually quite complex, requiring that the wires don't kink when the fridge is moved. Pete chats about the pluses and minuses of various appliances. We had chosen a conventional range top because I thought that smooth tops could be easily marred. Pete verifies that one has to be careful not to scratch them, and a special cleaner is required at $9-10 a pop. The smooth top was $200 more for a similar model. Later, though, I notice a cleaner in the supermarket for $3.

What Has Come Before?

Sometimes the job that has been done previously limits what can be done now, unless you are willing to pay the price. For example:

1. *The range had to be where its hookup was located. Therefore, the "dead" cabinets could not be resuscitated cheaply.*

2. *The medicine cabinets are rusty, broken and outdated. They have built-in lights that are too low for a modern overhead fixture, so we may have to get an exact replacement and forego style.*

During this whole week unpacking has been taking place. Bathrooms were scrubbed and rescrubbed, shower curtains and rods hung.

7/24

The carpet men arrive very, very early. I have learned that in this area someone may come to your door at 7:30 a.m., but it is considered

impolite to phone at 9:00 p.m. In a
few hours the men have carpeted the
bedroom. We have bed, chest,
dresser, night tables with lamps and
an armchair. Arnie touches up the
walls with paint where there are
nicks, holes, scratches and mystery
marks, in an effort to make the room
respectable until it can be painted.
Thick dirt has been removed from the
ceiling fan, and the broken
lampshades have been replaced with
new, modern shades.

7/25

Pete the Plumber comes. He
installs a hot water dispenser
(except for the electrical hookup)
and two updated bathroom faucets.
He will return after his vacation to
finish the sump pump installation by
creating a permanent place for it
where it cannot fall over.

7/27

We return to New Jersey to close
the sale of our old house. In the
late afternoon we go to Ikea for
lighting and Roman blind window
shades. They don't seem to have a
linens department anymore. They
have nice medicine chests but none
will fit beneath our light fixture

location without looking disharmonious.

7/28

I hang five Roman blinds, replacing the bed sheets that I had hung temporarily for privacy. Now we have a great view of the trees. I observe that in the time it took me to install the shades, the <u>Hometime</u> couple would have put a new addition on their house and created a modern deck.

We call Tommy about starting work on the garage roof.

7/29

There is an elegant wood railing on the stairway, all grungy with dirt and handprints. I work on this, cleaning with furniture refinisher, and sanding. I will stain it and protect it with polyurethane. I want to do this before carpet is laid on the stairway and landing.

We don't hear from Tommy. He is probably on vacation.

We decide to call the fireplace man. No answer, try Monday.

I get a garment rack, as I have no place to hang my clothes. I need one until we can buy a wardrobe. The post office made an attempt to deliver a comforter set, but we were away.

7/30

The new range has an odd, industrial smell and must be cleaned. The garment rack collapses and needs reassembly. I need a closet. I notice that the sump pump pipe is sending water about two feet from the house, where it is puddling around the foundation and seeping back into the basement. I see ants. Pete had intended to put in a new, longer pipe.

Unpacking continues. Arnie has had to do other work these past couple of days.

August: A roof over our heads; carpet beneath our feet

8/1

The fireplace dealer is quite tied up. I request a place at the end of his list. Someone will come to assess the fireplace in two weeks.

We want the septic system tuned up. One service talks about our system's never having been done right, and estimates a pump-out and repair for a minimum of $1,500-2,000, sight unseen. We decide to get a second opinion. We call the man who had been too busy in June to help. He'll be out to look at it next week. We figure if we get the same report we may have to go through with the job, but we are experienced with high estimates for elaborate jobs - sometimes you don't need granite counter tops when laminate will do the job.

8/2

We will want to buy light fixtures before Phil the Electrician comes, so we hurry down and get some. We buy a ready-made screen for the patio doors and take this with us. We also buy a ready-to-assemble

wardrobe and a tower of shelves for
books, all to be delivered. The
screen door is a travel disaster.
About a mile before we arrive home
with it strapped to the roof of the
car the screen door kinks. And it's
too short for the door. Luckily, we
bought the cheaper one. That's
about $60 down the drain this week
for the screen door and the garment
rack.

8/3
The past five days of rain have
intensified the smell of the old,
pet-stained carpets. I order new
living room carpet. Marion, the
Carpet Lady, lets me know that they
can recommend contractors if we need
any.
We get an appointment with Phil
the Electrician for Tuesday. It
looks as though he and Pete the
Plumber save Mondays for weekend
backlogs, so they are more likely to
have appointments available for the
other days.

8/4, 8/5
Hooray! We have a couple of sunny
days. I work on weeding the
driveway and paths. Arnie mows the
grass - hard work over the hill of

the septic tank. The new-mown grass smells wonderful. We let the pleasant smells waft across the stinky carpet. It'll be great when the carpet installers are done.

The wardrobe and book towers arrive. This is heavy stuff for the two drivers, who are only supposed to leave them at the curb. They tote the book towers upstairs.

Not a lot seems to be happening, but meal preparation and cleanup, laundry and bill paying must be done. We are also stymied by vacation time. The fireplace estimator, the main roof contractor and the plumber are all on vacation. The electrician has just returned from vacation. We are using this time for planning. We are discussing the composition of simple but extensive wall units.

8/6

Arnie assembles towers. I buy paints for faux finishing over the brown, photo-finished wood laminate bathroom vanities.

8/7

I call Tommy again. His wife says he is overloaded with work, but she will give him my message.

Norman the Carpet Man has not come to measure. I figure we need to make a more structured appointment than the loose one we have. I call and set a date and time.

Arnie assembles a closet for the guest room. I kibitz, helping slightly in balancing and attaching the knobs.

Another HUD Bid

A friend calls to say that a house in Rockville, Maryland, another area in which we have been interested, has appeared on the Internet as a HUD sale for $110,000 asking price. Arnie checks it out, calls HUD, and by persistence through the bureaucracy obtains the name of the broker who has the key. We get an appointment to see the house, grab maps, half a cup of coffee and drive 4-1/2 hours to Rockville, arriving in a sudden downpour. The house is represented as 4 bedrooms/1 bath. We can't see its color, as it is dusk. We are already acquainted with this neighborhood. The house is a doll house - living room, no dining room, dark paneling and cardboard ceilings, and a minuscule kitchen. The two upstairs bedrooms are small, windowless, merely a divided attic. The bathroom is old, the floor covered in badly matched vinyl tiles. The carpet is filthy and the house is dirty and smells bad. The windows are rusty and painted shut. The fridge is moldy, of course, but large and of recent vintage, the electric range looks okay, old 1940s metal sink with drain ridges, old wall cabinets still square, a hodgepodge of base cabinets, some not installed. Okay back yard. We think this is a good way to get into Rockville.

Our Realtor, Joe, has been nice enough to meet us at 8:30 p.m., having had to borrow a car since his was being repaired and coming from a neighboring city in pouring rain. He advises us that houses in that area have been selling in a few days, with five bids on them for more than the asking price. We ask what he would bid. His reply is "$115,000."

Arnie and I talk this over in our car. We think a cash bid for the asking plus a little bit may do it. We aren't willing to pay $115,000 for that house, so we bid $110,501 so that we won't lose it to the round number bidder. Joe offers to take 1% less commission so that we *have a better chance at it. He thinks our bid is an educated bid, but can't hazard whether we'll get it or not. We hope we'll get on the basis of prompt bidding, full price, and cash terms.*

We sign contracts, drive 4-1/2 hours back to Pennsylvania, because we have an early morning appointment with the electrician.

The following day we find we have lost the Rockville house to a bid of $132,000, 20% more than the appraised price. We wouldn't have bid such a price for that house in any circumstances. Actually, it's a relief, because the timing is bad - we're too busy handling serious defects here, so we would have had to pay holding costs on two houses while one or the other was standing idle.

8/8

Phil the Electrician installs fixtures and the hot water connection. The men think this is a very nifty device because they can avoid cooking and still have soup and coffee. A modern outdoor sensor light replaces a badly installed one. The new one is more modern, larger in keeping with the scale of the house and adds a lot to the curb appeal. The electrical work is just about done. We have had four hours of sleep, so we sack out for a couple of hours.

Tommy has not called.

The septic tank alarm goes off. We try to get our septic guy on the phone. All three of his lines are busy for hours. We call Roto Rooter. They tell us to go easy on the system, do no laundry.

8/9

Roto Rooter men arrive early in the morning, look over the tank. They think it is full and needs emptying, and fixing of the emptying conduits. The pump is okay. They return with equipment to repair the pumping conduits and have to go get jet equipment for pumping out the tank. It's done all in one day. The other major jobs have stretched out for two months. They suggest we have the holding tank pumped out next spring. Price was $450. The spring cleanup will be $450, less than the sight-unseen $1,500 estimate.

The living room has been measured for carpet at 7:30 a.m.

8/10

I ask for a newsletter at the development office, hoping to find an ad for a roofer. We find a builder who does roofs in this area. He will do a rubber roof on the garage roof deck. We ask about the other part of the roof. He suggests he can build up the rafters so that R-30 insulation can be installed, put in proper venting and ice guards and then install fresh shingles. He will give us an estimate later.

Can Amateurs Estimate?

We try to use R.S. Means Repair & Remodeling Cost Data 2000 to get an idea of how much the roof should cost. The rubber roof should be $4.96/sq.ft. @400 sq.ft, for $1,904. New shingles for the cathedral ceiling roof should be about $550, baffles for the vents $200, ice guards not listed, 2x2's for the rafter augmentation also not listed, insulation $550. We figure about $4,000 for all.

Henry the Builder comes in with an estimate of $800 for the rubber roof; $1,240 for a re-roofing with vents and ice guards, $2,480 for the

2x2 augmentation and insulation, total $4,520.

Although we arrived at similar totals, this shows we can't make good estimates. It may be because we can't break the tasks down correctly or that Henry's price is too high or that we haven't described the job correctly.

We decide to ask Henry to go ahead, with the caution that we think the price is too high. He could readjust down if it turns out that way, but we will pay his price at the end if that's fair. We do this because we think he is competent, based on intuition, and also looking at some additions he has done in our neighborhood. However, we don't actually discuss it with him this way, because we haven't decided what job we want, but ask him to go ahead with the garage roof right away, telling him we will decide later which of the additional jobs is to be done.

8/12

Doing the laundry is becoming a burden. The coin laundry is crowded most days, except at dawn on

Mondays, so we decide laundry equipment has become a priority.

The U.S. Post Office has sent us a newcomer's packet, which includes 10% discount coupons from Sears and Home Depot. Having previously had a long-lasting washer and dryer from Sears we decide to go to the higher price, after comparing. When we submit our coupon it is rejected because the appliances we want are on sale. No appeal helps. We feel we are being exploited and refuse the purchase. We choose from Home Depot's selection, but the computer is down, and although the floor sample labels the dryer as an in-stock item it is not in fact in stock. That would invalidate our coupon. The stockman is very busy with other customers, and closing time is approaching. Arnie will go alone tomorrow.

Buyer Beware

Read the fine print. Sears' coupon stipulated that the item not be on sale. Home Depot's coupon provides it be an in-stock item.

We pick wall units, but don't take them now, as we are too busy.

At home, we have a message from Marion the Carpet Lady that the living room carpet we chose would be $1,350 because of wastage in that particular carpet. She invites me to come in and adjust my choice, as I told her my limit was $1,000.

8/13

Arnie goes to Home Depot and arranges for a washer and dryer. Free delivery and installation are included, so we end up saving about $300 on the purchase. The sample labeled "in stock" was accepted for the coupon discount, even though it was not actually in stock.

8/14

Since we are going to be getting wall units and carpeting, I paint the wall that will contain the units. Arnie thinks we might be able to strike a deal with Norman - a $350 difference is a lot of carpet. The stairway can be pieced, and with a bit more carpet we might be able to come in with $1,500 for both the stairway and the great room.

8/15

We have to go to New York for medical and dental appointments. I stop in New Jersey and buy a comforter set for the new bed. The mail order set we received had not been as depicted.

8/16

We go to get Pennsylvania driving licenses and registration. Registration requires Pennsylvania insurance, which we have not yet applied for, but we do get drivers' licenses.

8/17

We are still really undecided on the roof job that Henry should do. Arnie asks him to go ahead with the garage roof part of the job, and we will make a choice between the other two jobs later.

8/21

Henry the Builder has scheduled the garage roof job for Friday. He will call the day before if he can't make it.

At this point we are inclined to do the re-insulation job because it would remove a perceived fault of the house and because we might get it back in reduced heating bills (we don't actually know the amounts).

I call Norman the Carpet Man again and leave a message requesting a new estimate.

8/22

My second plea for fireplace repair seems to have helped.

Dave the Fireplace Man will be here Wednesday to discuss the heating options.

8/23

I call Norman's again. Norman has been on vacation. Rob the Carpet Installer has stated that the Berber carpeting I chose will look stretched around the stairway ledges where it will be wrapped. It would have been $1,800, which Arnie and I decided would be okay after comparing prices in other standard carpet places. We're back to Square One, but we know a little more about the game. Marion will help.

8/24

Back to Norman's to select carpet. This time I have a sample of the tiles that will go into the adjoining kitchen, so it's easier to decide on a color. I go for the slightly more expensive soft carpet because the color selection is wider, and I can get a better match to the adjoining room. However, I pick the cheaper alternative in case something goes wrong with this estimate.

Dave the Fireplace Man arrives. He has some interesting options. We don't want to keep a wood-burning insert. Cutting wood and feeding the little stove which is there might be amusing at first, but it will soon be a big burden. If we put in a zero clearance fireplace it would be 80% inefficient, he says, because the damper has to remain open and heat is drawn through the chimney (does he mean 80% efficient?). Unvented gas logs would heat the whole house, 99% efficient. It would cost about $350 to install the unvented stove, plus another $225 to remove the present stove and paint the rear fireplace wall. There would possibly be other charges if trouble were discovered. A vented gas log fireplace is about $2,200.

Question: Would an unvented gas log system put moisture in the air? Dave himself has this system and does not find it to be a problem. Reservation: If it's unvented, could bad things happen? Solution: We will get a carbon monoxide detector. Either Dave or Scoot the Boss will call with an itemized estimate and schedule.

In the meantime, we have been very busy. Arnie spends a lot of time with the Motor Vehicle Bureau and car insurance company, inspection station, etc., but we're okay with cars in Pennsylvania now.

We have noticed a bus driving to New York City and have called that company. The representative is annoyed with my questions, can't describe where in town the bus station is located, just repeats the name of the town in which it is located. Later, when I went to a dentist, I found the bus station right next door. The street, although oddly situated, had a name, but the bus dispatcher didn't appear to know it.

Arnie now has reasons to do the cheaper roof job. He thinks the proposed buildup of the roof is unusual and isn't sure it will work. We can always amend later by applying the more usual solution mentioned in Reader's Digest

<u>Complete   Do-It-Yourself   Manual</u>, which is to put a second insulated ceiling below the cathedral ceiling. And then, of course, we wouldn't have to spend so much cash right away. I think I don't care either way because they are both good points.

Is This Sweat Equity?

Very little of the work done on this house so far has required our sweat.   The jobs we need here are really best done by pros.   Pumping out a septic tank with heavy machinery is not a do-it-yourself project.   The ladder required to reach the top of a 20-foot ceiling to install recessed lights is not common household equipment, nor does the average person have the license required for connecting circuit breakers to their electrical lines. True, I can do some of the painting, lay vinyl square tiles on a floor; Arnie can do difficult assembly of cabinets, level the washing machine. Most of our work involves planning what job is to be done, finding competent contractors and knowing how to deal fairly with them, arranging schedules, finding best

*bet furnishings.   Maybe it should be
called* programming equity.

8/24

We get an estimate from Dave the
Fireplace Man:

Remove, insert, clean firebox, replace damper	$225
New brick panels, back & bottom	100
24-inch gas logs	344.50
Install gas line	175
Total	$844.50

They can do it in about two weeks,
will call Monday or Tuesday to
schedule.

Marion the Carpet Lady calls -
yes, the carpet I chose has been
miscalculated.   Marion is a good
sales person with an artistic sense
of color, but really needs Norman
for the calculations; however, he is
on vacation.   The job will come to
$1,950.   This price is too far above
my mental budget of $1,400 - about
$900 for the living room and $500
for the stairway.   We go for the
cheaper one at $1,600.   They will
call next week to schedule.

8/25

Henry doesn't show up to do the roof. I call at 9:30 a.m. to "verify our 8:30 appointment," which is my way of saying, "Where are you?" He calls back at 11:00 a.m. to tell me his roofer has had an injury and they are all waiting to hear his doctor's verdict on when he can return to work. Monday is hopeful, the worst is two weeks. All materials have been purchased.

Arnie and I feel the repairs have been going too slowly. One reason is that we arrived at the height of the vacation season, when construction contractors are very busy here. Also, they go on vacation. Our usual sources are tied up, and we have spent time looking for new ones. Another reason is that we operate on New York time, and this is the country. As Arnie points out, nobody says, "I'll be right over." In this circumstance, we decide not to do things in series, one after the other, but to do things out of order or simultaneously, if possible, to catch workers. We therefore decide to call Kenny the Landscaper to do some of the painting, make landscaping plans and to lay plastic and a layer of gravel in the crawl space, especially since gravel will not be available in October. We will call Tommy the Carpenter again after Labor Day and ask for an appointment in the long future.

We have done nothing about the animal cage in the garage for a month. We have had one person try to play upon our fears of an unsanitary condition by talking about full cover fatigues, respirators and chemical fumigation, for at least $500, possibly more. I try not to have JERK written across my forehead. Other reactions have been, "Yew-wh," or silence. An Animal Cage Muse is not going to appear and do this job. This is a job for a wonder woman. Armed with dust mask, rubber gloves, rake, shovel, trash bags, whiskbroom and newspaper, I pry open the door to the cage and begin raking and shoveling. When I step into the cage I put plastic bags over my shoes. The job takes a few hours, but the cage is neat and free of any questionable debris. At this point it would be respectable to ask someone with a chain saw to dismantle the cage. Landscapers have chain saws. I'll add it to the list of jobs I would like Kenny to do.

Construction debris is becoming a problem. There is an individual garbage pick-up here, but the two companies that service this development will really only pick up a few cans once a week. I have been able to run outside with $5 and ask for a few more bags to be taken, but the accumulation is faster than the pick-up can handle it. Truckload pick-up for $50 is available, but the community forbids that size of pile in the yard (I'm glad of it, too).

Bad Smells

Most of the neglected houses we have seen smell bad, and this is one reason why they turn off so many people. If all a house needs is a little disinfectant solution to clean it up, it's a big bargain. Three of the houses we have bought were permeated with pet odors. In one, we merely had to discard the offending sofa (many cleanings could not get rid of Eau de Fido). In two others, the carpets reeked of pet excretions. The odors were so strong in this one that we found it necessary to replace the carpet as soon as possible, even out of logical order of work to be done.

Dampness is another reason for mildew smells. If the cause of dampness can be removed (wet basements, poor ventilation, overinsulation) the odors will often disappear.

Woodland animals living in the attic are another source. An extermination program for vermin may be called for. Where harmless animals are found, humane trapping and freeing them in a more appropriate environment can be done.

So if you think the situation is correctable, you may not want to summarily dismiss a smelly house.

8/26

A large part of the day is spent choosing paints and supplies and having paints made up in decorator colors.

8/27

The front door is rusty and had once been forced open.

It sticks a little, but we try to save it rather than get a new one for $400 with installation. Rust removers have been applied, then primer with stain killers and repainting, but the rust keeps showing through despite several applications. I sent for a substance that claims to turn rust into a black primer. It is very black. The paint is very white. Arnie makes several applications of paint, drying each coat with a hair dryer. It looks good. Let's see if it's stable. I had painted the outside with a color made to order, but it has a neon quality that doesn't really resemble the color I chose on the chip. I have a different brand made up and repaint the door. This is what we want.

What Did it Cost To Repair the Door?

1. *Three quarts of paint, primer and rust converter, a foam brush for each substance and some masking tape, about $45.*
2. *Nine hours of our labor (selecting, shopping, ordering, painting), maybe $180.*

If we had the job done by a pro, we still would have had to shop and select, find the pro, make arrangements, perhaps withstand postponement, with no recourse if we made the wrong choice of materials.

Conclusion: It cost $225, total theoretically - $45 in cash, actually.

8/28 - 9/4

All comes to a halt for the Labor Day holiday.

September: Carpet, yes; laundry room plumbing; heating plans go awry; fireplace installed; flower beds prepared; roof deal #1; electrical finished; master bathroom wrapped

9/5

I call the carpet installers. Yes, the carpet has arrived. Yes, they will install it tomorrow. I call Kenny the Landscaper. We have a tentative appointment for Saturday.

9/6

Carpet installers remove old, smelly carpet and install the new carpet. It takes all day, but things smell okay at last.

I call the roofer to schedule for next week. He tells me his injured man has not returned to work; if I can wait, he can do the job in two more weeks. I express my disappointment and mutter, "okay," trying not to be enthusiastic, but not exactly canceling either. In my opinion he knows he made an underestimate on the rubber roof and wants to extricate himself. Arnie is less skeptical. We will think it over.

9/8

The fireplace installers come to remove the broken wood stove. They find that the original floor of the fireplace had been removed and lowered, with a plywood floor installed below. Such a setup won't work for the gas stove we had in mind. They decline to take it out, preferring to wait for the final installation so they can avoid the double work of protecting carpets and moving furniture. I will have to call Dave the Fireplace Man. After consulting with Scoot the Boss, Dave faxes us information on the Heat'N Glo vented gas fireplace, which we originally had in mind. We are back to $2,280 for heat.

9/9

Kenny the Landscaper calls early to postpone. He has too much promised work to do. We make it definite for next week.

I leave a message with Cindy for Dave to call me back to put in an order for the vented gas log fireplace.

9/10

We were away since 11:00 a.m. No message from Dave. We are thinking that we are paying retail for our supplies. We'd like to find a way to obtain a discount. We will think about this and call Home Depot. I think we might qualify as a contractor.

I will call the fireplace man first thing tomorrow.

We put a date on the calendar two weeks from our last conversation with Henry as our deadline for hearing from him. We think it's up to him to make the move. If we don't hear by then, there are other sources we can try.

9/11

Dave the Fireplace Man isn't in today. Cindy isn't in either. They transfer me to Nancy, who will make sure the fireplace insert has been ordered and let me know.

9/13

Arnie has second thoughts, and calls Henry the Builder to make sure we're still scheduled for the new roof. Just in case Henry is avoiding us because of an underestimate of the cost of the rubber roof, Arnie offers him $100 more in an indirect way, so that he doesn't lose pride. Henry assures us he'll be ready at the end of next week. This date goes on the calendar, and this is the last postponement we intend to endure.

9/14, 9/15

We had decided that the kitchen floor was a priority because the carpet threshold couldn't be put in until the kitchen floor was laid, and the carpet edge might ravel if left raw. I lay the floor with the vinyl no-wax tiles I chose a few weeks ago. I change the metal threshold left for me by the carpet men for a wooden threshold. Arnie helps me lay it down. It looks classier, more finished. And what a relief that the floors are done - we can walk barefoot in any part of the house now without distaste.

9/16

Kenny the Landscaper comes with his assistant, Tom. They look over the jobs. It won't be possible to deliver gravel to the crawl space because there is no opening large enough to admit it. When the crawl space dries completely they will put in plastic as a vapor barrier and apply Drylok, a waterproofing epoxy. They will replace or fix a laundry room door. We decide which planting beds are to be weeded, turned over and fertilized. They laugh at my plans for a garden. I've ordered deer-resistant bulbs, but they think if the deer don't get them the woodchucks and squirrels will. We might try some Alberta spruce and Japanese *Pieris*, and lots of deer repellent. In their experience the deer are unreliable tasters and will suddenly attack a plant they have disdained for years. In my experience a one-foot folding fence will discourage woodchucks. Woodchucks don't seem to know how to deal with a fence and leave to try an easier way to get food.

Being helpful, Kenny and Tom mention contractors I might want to use. They mention Norman's Carpets and are pleased to know he has done all the carpets in this house. They also mention a roofer, Norm, after I say that our roofer has postponed twice. I am happy to have a name just in case, but at this point we are still committed to Henry. They assure me he is a no-games man.

Kenny will call me later in the week with prices.

9/18

A Home Depot Day. We decide it's time to get medicine chests and the light fixtures for them. We also order four knockdown bookcases for delivery. Replacement vanes for vertical blinds are on the list as well as some hardware, metallic paint, sample molding to try out. At the crucial moment, I can't bring myself to install a medicine chest like the old one. I get one I think is more in keeping with the modern decor. We'll just have to fuss with the position of the light.

I also remove a wallpaper border in preparation for repainting the bubble gum pink kitchen.

The Essential/Possible Method of Scheduling

Ideally, there should be a schedule and plan for doing jobs logically. For example, the plasterer should come before the painter, followed by the carpet installers. Things didn't work out that way. The carpet installers had to come first, because the old carpets reeked of pet odors. The carpet people arrived before the fireplace people came to remove the sooty wood stove because the wrong type of heating insert had been scheduled and the job had to be re-ordered. The roofer postponed twice, so we couldn't call the drywall people, so couldn't call the painter. The carpet threshold had to enclose the kitchen flooring, so the kitchen flooring was laid down before painting walls, in order to avoid wear and tear on the carpet edging. One wall of the living room was painted because wall units were needed so moving cartons could be unpacked.

I call this the essential and possible method of scheduling. Each job was done as it became essential and/or as it became possible.

9/19

I paint half the kitchen twice, once in white to cover the pink walls and once in the new cream color. The primer I had carefully saved and moved from the old house was hard as a rock, so I used one coat of cream paint as a primer. Painting takes an eight-hour day. An hour goes in spackling and taping; another hour in cleaning pans, brushes and rollers as well as removing both old and new goofs on the moldings. The pink color had been depressing, rather than cheerful. I know I won't have the energy to do this again tomorrow. Better wait a few days.

9/20

A day spent finishing up jobs I started and didn't finish: replacing the vanes on the vertical blinds with fresh ones and hanging a curtain rod and curtains on the largest living room window. I make a third attempt to hang a valance over blinds in the bedroom. I tape my six-inch level to a yardstick so I can get the rod aligned correctly, this time trying a wide width rod, but I fail again. This was a rod I had in my stock, but it's about an inch too short. I'll try a fourth time with a longer wide rod. It should be easier with the hardware already in place.

I call Pete the Plumber and Phil the Electrician. Pete calls back and we have an appointment for Friday to vent the dryer to the outside and to attach a filter to the cold water pipe in the basement.

9/21

Phil returns my call. We make an appointment to make an appointment next Monday, when he will know what his schedule is.

9/22

We haven't heard from the fireplace people. I think I'll call on Friday, but Arnie asks me twice, so I call today. They know nothing, but the boss will call me back.

9/23

Scoot the Boss says it will be here *next* Tuesday, and they will put it in first thing on Wednesday. Last week they said they expected it on Tuesday and would schedule me for the end of the week, but apparently they waited for me to call.

We hesitate to feel joy just yet. We believe they will be here on the stated day, but something could still go wrong.

9/24

Pete the Plumber comes early. He vents the dryer to the outside, instead of to the basement where it was adding excess moisture to the crawl space. He also installs a filter at the cold water pipe to remove the chlorine-bromine taste. The hot water maker at the faucet wasn't being used very much because the hot tap water had a bad taste, but now it will be filtered, too. This seems to complete the essential plumbing.

9/25

Unassembled bookcases arrive. We wanted these badly, as we hoped to make wall units, allowing us to unpack books that are still in cartons. We set up half the bookcases.

Kenny the Landscaper calls with his prices. He has a cold, and the skies threaten rain. We make a definite appointment for next week to do garden work.

Team or Gang?

When we started this project, I thought we had an excellent team lined up. From previous jobs we had a purchasing real estate agent, a selling agent, a plumber, carpenter, landscaper and handyman. Our purchasing agent has left real estate since we bought this house. The plumber came through. The carpenter was too busy. Ditto the landscaper and handyman, although he will come through later. Arnie points out that since the carpenter also does roofs, we would be hiding from him that we have hired a roofer. Since the drywall worker also paints, we can't tell him we already have a painter. Our electrician and plumber do know each other. But since they can't all work simultaneously, they aren't a team; they are more loosely connected - a sort of gang, actually, rather than a team.

9/26

Arnie has had tennis elbow, usually ascribed to repetitive screw driving, a likely diagnosis. Nevertheless, he insisted on doing the screw driving yesterday for fear that I, too, would develop a problem. Today his arm really hurts, and we'd better back off assembling.

I will weed and feed the lawn today, which has lots of plantain in it. Considering it was neglected for a long time it is not in such bad shape. A country lawn doesn't have to be as manicured as a suburban lawn, anyway. I really am thinking of a townhouse for our next house to avoid the lawn issue.

9/27

FIREPLACE! Well, almost. The fireplace installers, Marty, Ed, and The Gas Guy arrive. They spread cardboard boxes and a tarp on the new carpets. The old fireplace and chimney are cleaned out. The old broken stove is removed, and the gas log fireplace is installed. In the middle of this I step in and ask if everything is going as expected. Other than occasional checking or offering a cold drink, we like to stay out of their way until the end. They grin and tell us everything is great. Just as we leave, I overhear one man say, "The aggravation is just beginning." We clear out. Ed goes to the basement and installs the thermostat that goes with the fireplace. The facade doesn't fit, which seems a routine situation. They will take measurements for a custom-made facade, at no extra cost, which will be delivered in a few weeks. The Gas Guy makes a gas connection to the future tank.

They do a nice job and don't leave a speck of soot, which we consider to be very skillful. However, when they remove their cardboard they rip the door sweep. This may be a good thing, as it is rusty and bent, but I can't close the door. I decide to remove it all. Arnie has to help, as I seem to have a problem with okay conceptualization of the job, but inability to execute it. The door can close now, and we'll get a replacement sweep.

The only job remaining is to obtain propane gas into the gas lines. Here are the results of my inquiries:

Comparison of Gas Prices & Availability - 9/2001

Company A $2.05/gallon
Install tank and deliver in 3 weeks

Company B $1.45/gallon
$47 to install tank and deliver in 6 weeks

Company C $1.50/gallon
$75 to install tank and deliver in 2-3 weeks

We decide to take Company C because they can deliver, and their price is only 5 cents/gallon more than the cheapest. Additionally, our plumber has recommended them. In fact, when I call to sign up and I mention Pete the Plumber, they tell me the price is $1.40/gallon instead of the $1.50 they originally quoted, so we're okay on all counts. We have a definite appointment for three weeks from now.

I still have not actually finished fertilizing the lawn.

Arnie calls Henry, who gives another excuse and postponement. He is politely relieved of his obligation and thanked for his good advice. To his credit, he did not begin this job and then string us along with broken dates while he finished other jobs.

9/28

We are working too hard. We take a day off and go to the Bloomsburg County Fair, gorge on sausages and peppers, funnel cakes and a new delicacy, the blooming onion, a large onion cut radially into "petals," battered and deep fried. The exhibits of arts and crafts show enormous skill. The judges in the horticulture hall have written a card at each display telling the reasons for their decisions, thereby informing us of the standards of excellence. This was a nice break.

9/29

I finally finish fertilizing the lawn. I dig up some plants that seem to be good and store them in pails of water, to be replanted after Kenny and Tom work on the flowerbeds.

Arnie assembles another small bookcase.

Phil and his assistant install medicine cabinets with lights. Exposed lines in the crawl space are neatly and safely connected. Phil thinks the house has come a long way since we started.

9/30

Kenny comes with his assistant, Tom. In half an hour he has taken down the horrible cage, using hammers, pry bars and muscle. They weed the three garden beds, remove all debris, add a rich compost mixture and give planting advice. I thought they would use a Roto-tiller, but again they used shovels, wheelbarrows and muscle. Kenny comes with the phone number of Norm the Roofer.

I fill in around the new medicine chests with blue suede paint to match the rest in the master bathroom. This room is now the first fully finished room.

Master Bathroom Project

1. Clean dirty sink, toilet, vanity, bathtub, floor tiles, medicine chest.
2. Apply tile restorer to remove grunge on bath surround and tile floors.
3. Repair crack in toilet.
4. Purchase and install new toilet seat.
5. Remove old smeared paint at edges of bath surround.
6. Install flexible shower head.
7. Install new modern faucet.
8. Hang striped blue and gray shower curtain and liner.
9. Paint vanity dark blue suede over photographed wood original, clean inside and line with rubber-type shelf liner.
10. Spackle the hole where doorknob hit the wall, doorstop installed.
11. Paint bathtub back wall dark blue suede, the other three walls light blue suede.

12. Replace old, broken medicine cabinet and light with new, clean one of similar size, with light.
13. Seal holes in back of door with wood putty, clean door with furniture restorer.
14. Remove rust from drain ring and paint with metallic paint.
15. Remove old asymmetrical basic hook, replace with wrought iron decorative hook.

October: Get ready for spring; get ready for winter

10/1

I re-plant salvaged plants from the old garden: sedum, Cupid's dart, Echinops, lamb's ears and an unknown plant whose potential may be discovered in the spring. Its strap-like leaves suggest some sort of lily.

Arnie calls Norm the Roofer, who comes to evaluate the new roof job. He estimates $900 for a rubber roof. He and Arnie set 10/16 for the date.

10/3

I paint the remaining kitchen walls. This time I try omitting the primer step, especially because the new paints are said to cover in one coat. It seems to work. The finished walls transform the room. We scheduled this job rather suddenly, so I am off to buy paint for the wood-grain laminate wainscoting. By chance I happen on an overstock sale of black-front brand name dishwashers at 36% off. What serendipity! I buy one.

10/4

I paint the hall walls cream over the original bubble gum pink and do the kitchen wainscoting in a muted green. The shade dries a bit bluer than the gray-green it seemed in the can and on the swatch, but it's very nice and blends in with the new flooring. Now that cartons have been moved from the kitchen I can fill in the last three floor tiles. The kitchen project is going well.

10/5

I finish the wainscoting in the hall and paint the door to the garage. I feel as though I have put masking tape around the equator. Arnie says that is why the details look so good.

Painting: Things You Never See on TV

1. *Applying 8-1/2 feet of tape to molding in order to paint a rectangular panel measuring 4 feet by 3 inches.*
2. *Running back to catch drippy sections.*
3. *Removing masking tape, only to find that the paint has run under it in spots anyway.*

4. Removing masking tape, only to find you haven't painted close enough to the edge.
5. Rummaging among 15 brushes looking for the only kind that will suit, but finding you don't have that one.
6. Trying to remove the goof made by the previous painter and removing the new paint, too.
7. Running gallons of water over rollers, brushes, buckets and sponges to clean them.
8. Discovering a spot you missed after everything is neatly put away.
9. Painting your watch.
10. Cutting off the lock of hair you've painted.

10/7

The dishwasher is delivered. Pete the Plumber is needed to install it.

10/9

Samples show that if the decorative border is dropped two inches below ceiling height it looks better. Placing it right at the ceiling suggests that the rest of the wall is suspended from the border, which is not the effect we wanted. Applying the border doesn't go smoothly. Has anybody ever said, "Measure twice, paste once"? When I reach a corner and measure the next wall I realize I've done the wall to the left of the passageway at nine inches, and to the right of the passageway at 10 inches. I scramble to peel it off and place it correctly, but I tear a bit at the top in the process. Patching it works, but that was humbling. The rolls are said to contain 15 feet, but they don't. Three rolls are short one or two feet, leaving me shy. I have to return to the store and buy another roll. This one has 16-1/2 feet in the roll.

10/11

The border is finished, and it's a knockout. Apples and pears dance around the perimeters of the room.

Pete the Plumber comes to install the dishwasher, closing the gap in the base cabinets. Now there are all new appliances, a new floor, and painted and decorated walls. The only remaining ramshackle thing is the drywall gap over the range left from a missing range hood. The rest is decoration - new moldings and backsplash. Minimum work space and storage standards require another wall and base cabinet, but these seem a luxury. We'll wait and see if we need it.

The deer-resistant bulbs have finally arrived after numerous errors in the spelling of my name and my address, but UPS has finally found me. Arnie doesn't trust that these bulbs will grow, because there were so many mistakes, but I think this is cynical.

10/12

On Kenny the Landscaper's advice, the rich topsoil/compost that has recently been applied is not to be dug under to where the bulbs will be planted, because it is too rich. Arnie suggests mounding the topsoil to one side of the various trenches I will dig and mounding the natural earth to the other. It works well.

I can plant about 100 bulbs in one day before my back feels it. I want to be very careful not to hurt my back, so I don't push myself. I take out a birch sapling, which would grow into a tree and shade the pond if left to grow.

I devote this morning to going back over paint jobs, filling in missing spots near moldings, removing my goofs and the last painter's goofs. It takes about four hours, but the effect is much better.

10/14

In a few hours more I plant the balance of the bulbs, about another 100. This second digging unearths more rocks, and lets me loosen the soil further. I think I will have bulbs in the spring. Kenny's idea is that the soil amendments will diffuse down over the winter.

Arnie has obtained a new door sweep cut to size. It snaps right in without his having to remove the door, forming an even better seal than before.

10/15

We have spent $11,896 so far on repairs and improvements, as follows:

Amount Spent So Far	
Appliances	*$2,964*
Carpet	*2,904*
Electrical	*1,276*
Fireplace	*2,280*
Painting & floor tiles	*300*
Plumbing	*1,337*
Window treatments	*180*

Miscellaneous, such as	*655*
Hardware, screws,	
wardrobe and tips	
Total	*$11,896*

Arnie thinks if we had done this for business alone, we would have bought cheaper materials, such as cheaper carpeting, a more modest refrigerator and plain paint instead of suede paint. I'm not so sure. I think people will pay for style to a limit, the limit being what houses sell for in the neighborhood. I have tried to get comparable prices to houses like ours on the Internet, but they are not available for this area without a $1,000 subscription. A Realtor has mentioned that a 3-bedroom/2-bath house in this development readily sells in the high $70,000's.

I finish the last vertical blind spruce-up. Seven vanes are held onto the mechanism with copper wire because the attachments had been broken. To replace them, I take copper strands from an electrical wire Arnie has stripped for me and attach the new vanes similarly as the old ones were attached. Then the new vanes are measured and trimmed to size. It takes about two hours. When I'm finished they look a lot better, but don't work as smoothly as before. Would we have been better off to buy new ones? Custom-made blinds would have been much more expensive. If we wanted to buy ready-made blinds we would still need to cut the vanes to size, remove all the old machinery and drill new holes to install the new machinery. I think it's a question of taking the pains, which I didn't want to do on this task.

10/16

It's a rainy, misty day, so the roof won't be done today; in fact, probably not till Thursday or Friday, if the weather report is accurate.

10/19

Norm arrives with his equipment, but his helpers didn't show up. He goes back to get an extension ladder. The mystery of the huge difference in the contractor's book estimate and the actual roofers' estimates appears to be resolved: The type of roofing appropriate for this roof is a rubberized topping, not rubber. However, it can't be applied when the temperature is lower than 65 degrees, so he has obtained a similar one. It bears a warning that in California it has been found to cause cancer. We veto installing it. Fortunately, it can't be applied at temperatures lower than 65 degrees either. We go for a sealant, which will keep the roof tight until the spring. Norm will also apply flashing between the building and the garage roof so no water gets in, and he will remove the leaves and the soggy carpeting which has been so constantly wet that moss is thriving on it. When the roof has a chance to dry he will return and apply the sealant.

In the guestroom, I remove a vertical blind system, which is too bulky and large for the 10x10 space, spackle the holes and repaint where the brackets have been. I put up a roman blind and curtains. Now all the window treatments in the house are finished.

10/20

The gas company installs a 100-gallon propane tank behind the house, which they hook up to the gas line installed by the fireplace guys. The fireplace is lit, and *voilà!* we have gas heat.

Surprisingly, the gas flames are as interesting and colorful as are those from wooden logs, but they are more reliable and also more environmentally sound.

As long as Norm is here, and since he also does siding, he will replace some worn out window trim in the siding. He will also put some drip edges on the garage roof, a deficiency noted in the home inspection report. He will add drip caps to the windows flanking the fireplace, a deficiency he himself has noted. He also knocks out the depression in the chimney chase top so that water will not gather there and corrode the aluminum top.

Arnie thinks it would be a good idea to apply this sealant every year instead of having a new rubberized roof. I don't. I think it's just hiding wet plywood, probably full of carpenter ants rotting the wood. Arnie thinks there is no evidence of rotting wood, even though there are leaks. I agree to try it, but I do not admit there is no need for a new roof. The controversy here is that I think there has been structural damage, while Arnie thinks there has not.

The sealed roof looks very nice, smooth and level, with neatly applied flashing between house and roof. It is very reflective. We won't be able to walk on it for a couple of days. I think it will need some outdoor carpeting if it is to be used as a roof patio. I had in mind some roll-out cedar walkways. Maybe both.

We think we have learned a lesson from the roof matter. Had we gone to Home Depot in July to have the roof done the installation would have been accomplished more efficiently.

10/21

Ironically, it's a 75-degree day. Norm isn't here. I plant some Russian sage, hoping that the deer won't eat it. It is on a list of plants deer often disdain. The rest of our plant order will come later.

Arnie buys an auxiliary pump, hoping to pump out a sump that has never dried. He hopes that once it is dried the main pump will handle it. Otherwise, he will periodically go down to the crawl space and start the pump himself, emptying the water into the main sump.

10/23

I call Norm and leave a message on his machine asking him to return my call about finishing installation of the gutters, and more vinyl repairs on the siding.

I remind Arnie that we had decided to do the jobs in parallel, not series, so that we wouldn't have so much wait time. He replies that two trucks in the driveway will create a problem he doesn't want.

10/25

Arnie calls the drywall man, Vinnie, recommended by Phil the Electrician. Arnie thinks the jobs will call for $1,000. I estimate $500. The estimating book says $1.67/square foot. We make a list of the jobs to be done.

10/26

Vinnie arrives with his wife, Marian, and we go through all the items on the list. We have the remains of water streaks across some joists in the living room ceiling and elsewhere. Vinnie thinks these are moisture paths created by ice dams, and that we might want to postpone the retaping and plastering part of the job until we install ice guards. Arnie wants to take the risk of doing it before the ice guard job. He explains his theory that the streaks are a consequence of water condensation from the unvented gas heater used by the previous owners. An unvented heater releases the by-products of burning, carbon dioxide and water, into the air. Vinnie gently suggests he knows a roof maven, Jim, who can look at it. Arnie agrees.

So far we have the following opinions about the evidence of past moisture on the ceilings:

1. Install ice guards. The shingles can be lifted to do this and then put back. (1 person)
2. Install ice guards. No opinion on shingling. (1 person)
3. Install baffles, vents and ice guards. (1 person)
4. Use a couple of nails and install drip edges. (1 person)
5. Install gutters. (3 people)
6. Modify the heating system to eliminate moisture production. (Arnie)

As to the suggestion of the home inspector that the snow be shoveled off the roof, Vinnie and Marian think that's really funny because the sloping roof and the icy conditions would make this a treacherous job. The drywall job, including some painting, is estimated to be close to $1,000.

10/27

I call Norm's mother/secretary and explain that an anticipated large job had turned into a small job, and we could understand if he didn't want to continue, although we would like him to. I tell her if we don't hear from him by Monday night we will assume that he doesn't care to continue.

10/28

Norm calls and says he will continue, and Arnie tells him how delighted he is with his decision. Actually, we think he does an especially neat, thorough, and intelligent job. Later, he told us that he has jobs with builders to correct sloppy work in new houses.

10/29

Arnie and I discuss who will get the job if ice guards are required. Arnie thinks Jim, Vinnie's person, because Norm didn't think along these lines. However, Arnie points out, the gutters are a problem, because that has been promised to Norm or his associate. Now, acting in series seems better because if there are two roofers at once we are wrong, and the roofers are innocent.

Vinnie had wanted to schedule the drywall job for sometime before Thanksgiving, but this really upsets me because with a gaping hole in the ceiling of the downstairs bathroom I can't invite guests. We offer a rush fee. They don't say yes or no, but Vinnie will come on Election Day to close the bathroom ceiling. I assume the rest of the job will be done sometime before Thanksgiving.

We are not sure about getting a garage door sometime after the drywall in the garage is finished. The reason is unclear to me. If we do, it would be a good project to see if Home Depot can install it. There seems no point in having replacement railings and stairways done until the spring, as they will get weather-beaten.

In the meantime, we haven't been idle. Several days, not in sequence, have been spent trying to get an appropriate computer workstation for me so that my computer equipment and accessories can be organized. We have progressed to the point where a chain office store has agreed to send the station I want to their branch 30 miles away. From there I will have to either pick it up or persuade them to have a person with a van deliver it to me at my expense. The usual delivery sources will not deliver furniture to this area. At home, the components will have to be assembled.

We have removed a wallpaper border in the bathroom at Marian's request.

Arnie has been cutting the various cardboard boxes into flat pieces. They have accumulated from all the moving cartons and from all the appliances, plants and unassembled furniture. Now they take up a sizable space in the garage. He has taken many trips to the recycling center to dispose of them. Finally, the space is clear.

Many tote boxes have been purchased, filled and labeled neatly with their contents, and stored in the garage. These boxes are watertight, a necessity in the Poconos. Bit by bit, chaos in the garage is diminishing.

Leaves are being raked.

There is a bad smell in the downstairs bathroom, whose source we haven't located. I think it will be better when the bathroom ceiling is closed up.

10/30

No Norm. Arnie sets about fixing the laundry doors. We had bought two 30-inch tracks and hardware to serve for the 60-inch track, which was not in stock, thinking to replace the malfunctioning one. The doors have been leaning against a living room wall, and we'd like to clear them out. Arnie fixes the doors, using hardware from the bifold track box.

Norm calls and says he will definitely be here tomorrow at 8:30.

The new fireplace uses electric power to run its blower. Power outages are inevitable. We will augment the main system with the unvented wall gas heater. We call the gas supplier, who says they can hook it up to the tank in two weeks.

10/31

Norm arrives at 11:00 a.m. He doesn't have any of the equipment he needs to do the job and will have to get it. He takes measurements, which he seems to have difficulty remembering. I take them down on a pad for him. He has a dental appointment at 2:00. He goes to get his equipment and to meet his dentist. He brings the equipment, then goes home at 3:30. He says he will be back tomorrow at 8:00 or 8:30.

November: Drying up

11/1

We leave at 11:00 a.m. to pick up a computer workstation 30 miles away. When we return at 2:00, we find Norm has apparently been here and left some equipment. He pulls up in his truck a few minutes later and begins work on a gutter. At about 5:00 he leaves, as it is getting dark, says he'll be here tomorrow at 8:30 a.m., to put in a full day. The gutter and leader system he has installed is an excellent job - neat and straight. The edges of the house look more finished.

11/2

Norm arrives at 10:45, works for an hour, goes to get an essential part which he thought he had but doesn't. Then, working steadily, he installs another gutter and leader, finishes drip caps on two windows, repairs the pet hole in the siding and the shot vinyl around a window, all nice work. However, while on the roof he notices many nails protruding through the shingles and some popped plywood. This opinion is more believable than the others are because he is the only one who has actually climbed the roof. His estimate for both roofs (the sloped ceiling roof and the hall/bedroom roof) is $2,200, high estimate. He asks if the inspector made any recommendations. In fact, he did: he suggested that we could get the snow shoveled off the roof in the winter. Norm says that costs $200. Arnie wants to think about the new proposal. Arnie decides he will wait until the roof leaks, then have it done rapidly, because we learned by asking around that anyone we knew who ever had a new roof installed had leaks that needed repair after the new roof was made. I am laughing about "rapidly," having seen that with luck this means about two weeks. I will be happy if I'm wrong.

Arnie has prepared an extra $50 for Norm because we realize he came to do a $900 job which turned into a smaller job. We were able to work the whole job of odds and ends into $550: roof coating, vinyl siding repairs, drip caps, drip edges, gutters and leaders. These should leave us drier all around.

I am urging Arnie to take a few days off and rest his arm. I also think he needs refreshment, as he has responsibility followed by responsibility.

11/6
We go to New Jersey to get our winter clothes from storage.

11/7
Vinnie is here at 7:30 a.m. to begin drywalling the small inside jobs. The bathroom ceiling is finally closed. The room smells bad. Arnie runs a fan for several hours, and there is some improvement. He also shuts the bathtub drain and runs some water into the tub to test the theory that the bad smell is emanating from the bathtub drain. Vinnie wants to come at 7:00 a.m. from now on. This is not exactly my best time, but I'm glad he is doing a job that de-sleazes the walls, so I cheerfully consent. That night I sleep in the clothes I will wear the next day and set the alarm for 6:30 a.m.

11/8
Vinnie arrives at 7:07 a.m., with his joint compound already mixed.

We are all feeling woozy from the bizarre election results.

Arnie has been talking to Vinnie about the roof insulation problem. Vinnie agrees he wouldn't have consented to construction of the 2x4 bridges that had originally been proposed. It's not clear that it would work, and we would be going to unusual construction. In the evening, Arnie talks about scheduling a trip to Maryland, but he seems to be including in the plans a decision to have Norm install a new roof. I am actually delighted.

11/9

Vinnie arrives at 7:00 a.m. for the final coat of joint compound. We are to do the light sanding. Arnie talks to him about putting insulation board under the present ceiling as a solution device which was mentioned in the Reader's Digest New Complete Do-It-Yourself Manual for adding insulation to already-built houses. Vinnie thinks its benefit is doubtful, and it's very expensive. I'm relieved, because I think it would uglify our cathedral ceiling, but I would have had to consent to a prudent method if it would work. He suggests putting the ceiling fan on low. Actually, that's too noisy. He says if he doesn't get in touch with us by Thanksgiving to continue the work, we are to call him.

There is a dark red candle wax stain on the stone fireplace hearth. I try ironing it, then scraping. It doesn't help. Neither does icing it. I try rubbing it with a Carborundum knife sharpener. This takes most of it out, but not all. Acetone doesn't work. I have tried stone cleaners in the past and found them to be ineffective.

We had thought that Kenny the Landscaper would paint the high-ceilinged rooms. He has ladders and has done this sort of work for us before. However, Vinnie had included painting in his price for taping and replastering the loosely taped joints on the living room ceiling. It is now apparent that he is the one with ladders and will have moved the furniture for drywalling and plastering, so he is the one for this job. It will be more efficient to move furniture and place drop cloths only once. For $200 he will paint the hall and bedroom, too, where he is also working.

But I think it is important to provide work for Kenny. He has been willing in the past to do unusual jobs it would be hard to hire out. We think we have just the thing for him. We have been buying some unassembled furniture, and the repetitive action of driving screws is one reason why Arnie has tennis elbow. Kenny is in condition for physical work. We have a computer desk, some small storage units and will buy a tall kitchen pantry closet that will require assembly. We will see if Kenny might be interested in this job.

11/11

Now that the ceiling is drywalled, I paint the downstairs bathroom. I define a room as having a ceiling, four walls, a floor, and perhaps a window and doors. At last, all the inside rooms are *bona fide* rooms.

Painting a small bathroom should be easy, but it's not. Most of the job is composed of cutting around corners, painting around the sink, toilet tank, shower surround, heater, baseboard moldings and doors.

11/12

I slept almost 12 hours. Today is a bad tool day for me. When I try to remove the tiny screw required to disassemble the towel bar so that the base plates can be installed, I can't budge it. I have to ask Arnie to do it for me, and then he does the whole thing.

I want to hang a nine-drawer bathroom wall cabinet for extra storage. The screw provided doesn't fit into the wall anchor provided. I get a bigger wall anchor, which makes a large hole in the wall, and the anchor falls through. I patch this hole with wall patch and joint compound, but I know it won't hold another anchor. The cabinet had been carefully centered to both the toilet tank and the medicine cabinet. A different spot won't do it. With difficulty, Arnie puts one drywall screw through each of the nine compartments so that its weight is distributed — sort of like laying it down on a bed of nails. An ingenious solution, and the cabinet looks lovely.

11/13

The market for houses has been
going wild in Rockville, Maryland,
where we had made our bid in August
for a HUD house. There are no
longer house sales near $100,000
cited in The Washington Times sold
lists. If we are lucky we may be
able to get a townhouse or condo in
a small neighboring city for a low
price. We will go there this
weekend and explore. We have lists
of data of recently sold HUD and VA
houses, with addresses. This should
constitute a feasibility study.

The gas company hooks up the
unvented wall heater. They agree we
need a bigger tank. They will come
this week, before we need more gas,
and install two vertical tanks
instead of one large horizontal
tank, which would take a lot of room
on the patio and uglify it. The
same man who came today had
installed the tank and hooked it to
the gas log fireplace. He is very
proud to see it working and pleased
that I remember him.

Arnie notes that there are two
areas in the small downstairs
bathroom that have never been
caulked: the toilet and the gap
between the bath surround and the

tile floor. Not long after he caulks the toilet the bad smell we had been working on with fans and deodorants goes away.

11/14
To Home Depot for odds and ends - some molding to practice cutting, knobs and pulls for various cabinets we have assembled and new wall plates.

11/15
Using the Internet, I try to get cheese leaves, decorative paper leaves on which cheese and other appetizers are served. They will be used on the newly painted bathroom walls, to create an effect of falling autumn leaves. The first order bears a message stating there is an error in the order, so I resubmit the order. Then I get notice of two orders and have to arrange to return one. This is a consequence of rapid response at electronic speed — you don't get much of a chance to think about it.

11/17-11/19
We drive to the Washington, DC suburb, hoping to see mainly sold houses (we have bid statistics from

HUD) and two from the Veterans Administration, two that are for sale according to www.iown.com. We get directions for our itinerary from www.mapquest.com.

There is one likely townhouse for sale, and we know of a comparable house for it two blocks away in the same development for $35,000 more. It is a better construction, however, sided with brick and cedar shingles. I don't see that this is a good value financial transaction, though. Suppose we got it at the $69,000 asking price (in this market we might have to pay more). There would be about $2,000 buyers' closing costs, about $8,000 estimated to fix it. If we were to sell it, we would have to pay a $5,000 commission to the real estate agent. This comes to $15,000 in expenses. Adding to the purchase price, the total is $84,000. The comparable house is for sale for $104,000, but it has more desirable features, such as a brick and cedar shingle exterior, and this is only looking at the outside. I estimate that at most we could make $10,000 cash, which wouldn't pay much for our labor.

A more upscale neighborhood in this city that neighbors Rockville seems very nice, but I think that since the city consists largely of townhouse developments, an investment house will be limited by the price that is typical for the development it is located in. Robert Irwin, in his book <u>Find It, Buy It, Fix It</u>, has mentioned this aspect of development houses as risky investments for fixing up. We wouldn't want to live here because the city is composed of development after development, with strip malls tucked away here and there, contributing to the lack of a homelike ambiance.

We look at one house in Rockville. It is a 2-bedroom/1-bath house, 692 square feet, in a swell location near a Metro to Washington, DC. In New York, those little houses would be quickly occupied by artists. This house, however, is next to one piled high with junk and autos, which could be a disaster. We have read that a fence will cure all in this situation, but we think it won't cure loud boom boxes, barking dogs or bad attitudes. Interestingly, it is the same price as the best townhouse we saw this weekend in the upscale neighborhood, with the same square footage. In any event, it is sold. We decide the Rockville location is more convenient to Washington and to certain features in Rockville that can be expected to expand, and that we will do better by paying more in Rockville. We also think we won't be able to get a house through HUD in the location we want because potential foreclosures can easily sell in this hot market via private means. We therefore will find an agency whose ads indicate they know what a fixer upper is and have some small stock of such houses.

But we still have major repairs here to get our present house under control, such as the plaster and paint, and the roof. We won't act until January.

11/20

The leaf "wallpaper" project is difficult. As soon as the wallpaper paste hits a leaf, it curls up. After a few trials we hit on a method. A thick layer of paste is placed on the wall. Then a thick layer of paste is placed on the leaf. This is smoothed out with a damp sponge, and a wallpaper spatula is passed over it carefully to get out the excess paste. After several hours of artistic placement and careful application of the six different types and three colors of leaves, the job is done. I develop decorator's remorse. There is too much decoration, I think. Arnie thinks it has a lot of impact. I think it has too much impact. We'll wait and see. When the more subdued shower curtain is hung, it tones down the leaves. I like the effect a lot. Now I hope they will all stay put.

11/21

A few leaves that are located near the electric heater are loosening. I repair them. Some are okay, but the paste on two of them dries out, and they won't stick. I plan to redo these in the spring, when the heater is off. Then the paste will have a chance to dry slowly enough.

11/22

Some leaves are actually falling. Arnie figures out they probably have a coating, so as not to stick to the cheese. Therefore, we should use border paste, which is meant to apply a border to vinyl wallpaper. In this case, the backs of the leaves are functioning as vinyl wallpaper. The border paste works.

Our friend in Arlington, Virginia sends us a recipe for his mother's onion biscuits and an article from the local newspaper that a genetics laboratory is contemplated in a city near Rockville, which would add more value to the real estate there. But actually the main matter is that we would not like to live there. I make the biscuits. They are excellent.

11/23

On Thanksgiving weekend we have a reservation at an elegant restaurant, a restored historic railway station. Arnie has the flu, but we go anyway. It's an all pleasure experience - swell food, live music, good drinks, and beautiful people. Nice holiday.

11/24

I get the flu. All muscles feel like rubber. Febrile attempts to get working are useless. We surrender.

11/26

I cut pieces of baseboard clam molding, which I had prepared by sanding lightly and staining, to replace pieces that are inexplicably missing from various locations in the living room and the guest bedroom. Some pieces don't fit exactly, because the moldings change profiles as they turn corners. For example, the kitchen molding is a three-inch baseboard, but the living room molding around the corner is two-inch clam molding. I fashion transitions with wood putty already stained with the same color as I had stained the molding. The finished product is a more complete look. I will continue this project when I feel better.

11/27

We ran out of propane, despite our call last week to the gas company and their assurance that we were on their route. An early morning call, and we are assured that we'll get it today. By 3:00 p.m. we still haven't seen anybody. Another call - Bob of the gas company is exasperated because we haven't been scheduled at all. He will send someone over. At 4:30, we've received gas. The bill is not too bad at $304 for the month, and it's been an unusually cold October and November. We've been using electric heat as a backup, closing off unused rooms with the electric heat at 55 or 60 degrees, putting the thermostat down to 60 degrees if we expect to be gone for a few hours. The electric bill is $115.

I call and leave a message for Norm reminding him to pick up the debris he was going to get last Saturday and asking him to call me.

I call Vinnie for an appointment to continue with the drywall in the garage. He picks December 11. The late date shocks me, but then I remember he had done the bathroom ceiling quickly as a favor. I gladly agree.

Norm doesn't return my call.

11/28-30
We continue to suffer with the flu, malaise taking over and weakening us.

11/30

I call the fireplace office to find out about the progress of the better-fitting facade. I talk with Dave the Fireplace Man. He doesn't remember the sale and doesn't seem to know the insert I'm talking about. Further, I realize he doesn't know what *facade* means. I apologize and explain that it's the front surround of the firebox. He says he'll get back to me. I think this means trouble.

Norm may not know it, but he has till this Saturday to get in touch with us. Otherwise, we are thinking of giving this job to Home Depot and hiring a carter/handyman to remove the debris. My cousin in Arizona e-mails me that she has used Home Depot to install a new kitchen in her house and that the contractors were eager to please because they wanted the Home Depot business.

We have two inches of snow.

We feel lousy - snuffling, coughing and muscle cramps. Surely, we'll get better, but it doesn't feel like it today.

December: Final fireplace; about tin ceilings; guest bathroom complete; garage drywall; trash collection; wildlife hunting; moldings; guest room complete; next year's tasks

12/1

The fireplace office calls to ask if Wednesday morning is okay to install the new facade. It sure is.

12/2

I return the call to the fireplace people to confirm the appointment with their receptionist, Felicia.

12/3

We have sent for a catalogue for tin ceiling tiles because we would like to use them as a kitchen backsplash, which is now made up of an unsophisticated tileboard. There is unfinished drywall behind the range, where it appears a range hood had been wired. We saw the tin tiles advertised at the back of a remodeling magazine. An 18x48" stainless steel tile backsplash costs $75.00. We will need four, and there is a $20.00 minimum shipping cost. The cost seems out of proportion to this kind of house. It might not be a good do-it-yourself job for us because we don't know how to handle this material. We think we might apply it over the range wall only, because a nonflammable material is needed. The sink wall can be done in heavy textured wallpaper, much easier to handle, likely to be successful, and paintable. We want to do more research about this material. I have seen tin tiles loose in a Home Depot in Paramus, New Jersey. We'd rather buy one or two panels at a time, and I believe I saw 30"x30" panels there, much easier to handle.

12/4

We return from a trip to New York. A sample board of roof shingles is leaning against our stair railing. Apparently, Norm is still on the job. Of course we would like to have him do the roof, but it isn't 100% certain that he was the one who left the shingles. We don't really think it was the Roof Muse, but we will wait until we hear actual words from Norm. It is too awkward to call and ask if he meant for us to select shingles.

Arnie is thinking we will just have Vinnie go ahead with the repair of the ceiling. If Norm shows up in that time and wants to do the roof, he may have to work simultaneously with Vinnie. Arnie also suggests Vinnie may be able to hang the backsplash.

12/5-12/7

Moping around with this cold, trying to do little things like trim the carpet underlayment to fit better, putting epoxy plugs into holes where the former range hood was attached.

The fireplace company brings a better-fitting facade for the gas log fireplace. Later, there are some chemical smells which we think are coming from the new finish. An on-off switch in the frame is missing. After we're sure the odors are coming from the new finish and have burnt off, I'll call to have the switch supplied.

We talk about the roof again. I am not insistent on this matter, but I do want to have reasons that satisfy me, rather than avoid the issue. Arnie says his view is that it's not such a great idea to have it done in this cold weather. It's not an emergency, there are no visible leaks despite torrential summer mountain rains, and he will accept a couple of leaks so that it can be done right in the spring, even if we might have to repair some of the living room ceiling. I absolutely disagree with this, because I see a few water stains, but he thinks they are either from former leaks before there were any drip edges, or condensation from within.

12/8

I finish the bathroom project of affixing my paper leaves with border paste. The first floor bathroom is finished.

First Floor Bathroom Project Summary

1. Clean and scrub.
2. Replace an ugly faucet with new, modern one.
3. Affix loose tiles with matching grout.
4. Line vanity closet with shelf lining cut to fit around plumbing lines.
5. Antique crackle glaze dark-paneled vanity.
6. Caulk toilet, sink, bathtub-to-floor gap, and surround-to-wall gap.
7. Install a medicine chest — have old one removed and new one recessed into the wall.
8. Put new light over the medicine chest - obtain a fixture, have old light removed, connection for new light installed at a correct height.
9. Hang a shower curtain - obtain curtain and liner, buy and assemble the rod, install the rod.
10. Remove the old wallpaper border.
11. Arrange to have a large hole in the ceiling drywalled.
12. Paint the bathroom.

13. Remove an unaligned towel rack. Choose a new rack and install it correctly.
14. Order paper leaves, correct order, affix them to the walls.
15. Remove the old clothes hook, shop for and install a more decorative hook.
16. Putty and sand various holes in door.
17. Purchase and hang an additional storage cabinet.
18. Sand and stain base moldings.
19. Remove old pink paint from the bath surround.

Shop till You Drop

Many tasks that can be described in one line actually require extensive shopping. Consider some of the items in the bathroom project:

Shopped for cleaners in a supermarket. Realized I needed a grout restorer, a product usually available in mail order catalogues. Ordered it, waited for it, was home to receive it.

Grout. Couldn't get a small amount, had to ask advice in Home Depot. They could only suggest using part of a big package. Had to *do the math to mix a suitable amount.*

Bought shelf lining.

Shopped for paint for the crackle finish. It wasn't available in the brand I chose, had to work it out with other brands.

Obtained the faucet for the plumber to install.

Shopped for shower curtain, liner, tension rod.

Purchased caulking in shade to match bathroom fixtures.

Old medicine chest was an odd size. Went to home stores and to Ikea several times. Didn't want the only one available in that size and decided to bear the expense of installing a totally new size.

Shopped for a new light fixture. Shopped the catalogues for a towel rack to match the faucet.

Shopped for paint and accessory supplies such as brushes, trim rollers, spackle.

Looked for cheese leaves on the Internet. Found and ordered. Error message appeared, so I placed the order again, found two thank you's on my e-mail and discovered that both orders had been filled. Returned one, completed application and drove to the post office with the excess order.

Trip for wallpaper adhesive. Return trip to buy border adhesive.

Shopped for decorative door hooks.

Looked in several kitchen departments for a spice cabinet with compartmented boxes to serve as extra storage. Found actual storage cabinet with compartmented boxes while shopping for other storage units.

12/9

I drive to buy baseboard and moldings to replace the missing trim in the kitchen and hall. A miter box and saw are provided. Customers cut the length they need - or the one that will fit into their car. I also buy decorative knobs for the assembled closet and splash block to extend the new leaders farther from the house.

12/10

We've been at home too long. We make this a movie day. Unbreakable was fascinating.

12/11

Vinnie arrives at 8:00 a.m. with his wife and an assistant. By noon they have reinsulated and correctly drywalled the garage ceiling. The only hitch is one plumbing pipe that extends a few inches below the ceiling. We agree to insulate it and apply duct tape, beauty not being the issue in this functional space. Vinnie also gives me the name of a trash removal person, sorely needed now that we haven't seen Norm in more than a month.

Arnie and I work on the hall baseboard moldings. We're having a tough time using a hacksaw in our miter box. Also, the molding is taller than the box, making it hard to start accurately. I do the geometry wrong on two pieces. One is saved, the other wasted. We are having trouble coping a curved line on a tiny piece of trim to mimic the complement of the adjoining baseboard. I think part of the trouble is that it's a tiny piece. The other problem is the saw. It seems to take a long time to saw the wood. I go out and buy a new backsaw, which is really the correct tool to use in a miter box, and a sanding drill attachment. They are a big help.

12/12

Dennis the Carting Company Owner calls. We have an appointment for Friday at 10:00 a.m. for him to pick up the trash. To give me an idea of his price he tells me the dimensions of his truck, and his price per truckload. Since I know how much debris I have I can make my own estimate.

12/13

I have seen a picture of a nice kitchen trashcan, but it's in a gourmet catalogue and has a gourmet price. I have bought a 20-gallon metal trashcan, which I prime, paint in a cream color, and accent the raised portions on the lid in blue-green. It looks nice. I paint a matching stripe around the can, but do a bad job of it. The concept is good. I will repair it tomorrow.

12/14

One day last week I noticed a really bad glue job on a filler strip in the kitchen cabinets. I touch it gently, and two strips fall out. They had never been screwed in. I sand off lumps of glue with #40 sandpaper, then gently sand with 150 grit. They look better already.

I see that one of these boards won't be easily screwed in. If it had been screwed in before the facing cabinet was put up it would have been easy, but it won't be possible to get a screwdriver into that spot. I glue it well. I don't have a clamp that will fit, so I use duct tape to hold it tightly till the glue dries. Maybe I'll try to screw it in somehow. We like to avoid a careless job if we can help it.

I had sent for an address plaque that stakes into the ground. The siding or the metal door would have to be drilled to get numbers onto the house, so this one was more suitable. However, the ground is frozen. Another spring project. I think the plaque is quite elegant.

I paint over the runny blue stripe on the trashcan. This time I will let it dry overnight, then use blue tape to define the stripes better.

12/15

The stripes look nice. The can is not as refined as the one in the catalogue. It's more arts and crafts-like, but then it cost $25 for the materials: can, tape, paint and brush, with free labor, instead of $95 ready-made.

At 11:30 a.m. the carting company men call to say they were delayed in New Jersey and will come at 2:00. They arrive at 3:00, drive right past the house. I flag them as they come around the block again. They remove $65 worth of construction debris. I am delighted because:

1.   Nobody likes garbage in front of the house.
2.   I don't have to nag Norm about it. This leaves us free to nag him about the roof. I will try to call Sunday night, a time I find most people home, as I don't want to leave a long message.

I glue the cabinet filler strips in place to dry overnight.

I redo the painted stripe on the trashcan, then realize the trash bag will cover it when it's in use. I will add another stripe. I will try to think twice, do once.

12/16

I can manage at least one well-placed screw in the filler strip. It looks much better without the lumps of glue filling in the tiny gap. I may have placed it better than it was originally done.

12/17

I cut the last piece of hall molding, stain all the pieces and set them to dry in the garage.

I call Norm, who is at home with a bad flu. I tell him that I'm calling to verify that the roof shingle sample was his and that he meant for us to choose a color. He says that he had attached his card to it, but it probably blew away. I tell him what color we want. He explains that he hasn't been able to get helpers willing to work, but he hopes to do so in the spring. We agree to speak in March if the weather is good, April if it's warm by then. I tell him he doesn't have to worry about collecting the debris. He apologizes. I feel better about our deal.

12/18

We hear odd noises on the landing. A ground squirrel is in the house. We hope to open the front door and push it out with a broom. It is very cute, but it can't live here. It scurries in its own direction, heads toward the sink and then disappears. I close all doors, put away the dinner dishes and all food. We find that the soffit at the landing has a large hole in it. I don't really think animals live here, because there is no animal odor, but we cover the hole just in case.

12/19

I call pest control and am referred to a wildlife control person. He doesn't return my call.

I work on installing new moldings. The larger pieces look good, but the small coped piece doesn't withstand hammering or nailing, and it breaks into three pieces. I reassemble it and trace its outline. Using a coping saw is slow work. After two hours, the new one is only half done.

12/20

Since we see no further sign of this cute animal, we think it may have wandered in when we had the doors open to set up a pump. I won't pursue the wildlife control man just yet.

12/21

After an 80-mile drive to Paramus, I get to handle the tin ceiling tiles. They are sturdier than I imagined. Some are priced at $3.95/square foot, others at $8.15/square foot.

12/24

I am definitely going into some kind of hibernation, moping around, taking a long time to do simple tasks. I finally change the knobs on the armoire to handles. The single knob showed the spackle fill-in too plainly. Now the guestroom is complete.

Summary of the Guestroom Project

1. *Have electrical circuit line brought to room.*
2. *Dust and wash walls, vacuum carpet.*
3. *Prime walls free of graffiti, spackle numerous holes.*
4. *Paint bubble gum pink walls a cream color.*
5. *Arrange for removal of pet-stained carpet and replacement with new, arrange to have doors cut to accommodate the new carpet.*

---

6. *Wash windows, remove stickers and glue from windows.*
7. *Obtain new screening, remove torn screening, and replace with new.*
8. *Choose armoire for use as closet, order, wait for delivery, and assemble closet.*
9. *Choose and install new knobs to replace industrial style knobs on closet.*
10. *Cut, stain and install missing base trim.*
11. *Have carpet people trim a door they missed the first time.*
12. *Remove vertical blinds and machinery, spackle and paint old holes; install decorative curtain rods, curtains and roman blinds.*
13. *Purchase nested tables as night table, furnish with bed and bedding, small chest of drawers, bookcase, wicker chair and ottoman, lamp.*

The coped molding is really tough to do. On the chair rail one nail won't go all the way in, yet it won't come out. A wrench doesn't work. Arnie uses another wrench to give it leverage, and it comes out. Physics rules. Eager to finish the coped molding piece, I hold the back saw while Arnie passes the coped piece over it, and it is finally cut out. It fits well, and I glue it to the wall and to the piece at right angles to it. I have just enough wood to redo another tiny piece which I had done sloppily. All the hall base moldings are now done. I think I have enough practice now to put up some long chair railings.

We hear a sound from the upstairs landing as though furniture is being moved. Is this Supersquirrel trying to remove the drywall lid Arnie placed over the hole? The drywall lid is still in place, but with a mirror Arnie finds a second hole against the wall that he didn't notice before. He puts a carton of reference books next to it. We will page the wildlife control guy after Christmas.

12/26

We plan another feasibility study, this time in College Park, Maryland, which we will combine with a New Year's holiday in Washington, DC. College Park is a college town of the University of Maryland, located along the Washington Metro and not far from the city. We will look in on Rockville once more.

12/27

We think that a professional animal control solution would be expensive and inquire about doing it ourselves. Yes, a squirrel can be released in the nearby state park. An Internet site suggests repellent pellets followed by repellent spray, or a live trap. We don't want to use poison for humane reasons, but also because dead animals smell. I can only find the repellent spray with difficulty. Arnie changes his mind about doing it. We decide to wait for a second episode, as our complaints are too vague.

12/29

We go to Washington for a working vacation to investigate College Park. Rockville is now out of our reach. The cheapest house, according to Internet sources, is $139,000 for houses in rundown neighborhoods or on busy streets, where $100,000 or less was a common price last year. Is this the peak? It's a speculation. Especially with the volatile stock market, we are not looking for a speculation.

College Park is a quiet town—mainly small houses, bungalow style. One expensive section is University Park, according to the map. The question here is If house prices run in a narrow range, does it pay to buy a fix-up? Maybe a very small profit can be made. Only 28 houses were for sale on the multiple listing from the Internet, no government foreclosures.

We will go on hold, get our present house in better shape. Everything moves so slowly. I think we could go faster if we were not so particular about the fine points.

We have been waiting for Vinnie to finish painting before we call Kenny about assembling cabinets and the computer station, but Vinnie does one job, then waits a few weeks before he begins the next phase. We've been waiting since early November to get a week's work done. He did a terrific painting of the bedroom, then wants us to call next week to schedule the living room. We thought he would come the next day. I would have begun arrangements for the new garage door, but Arnie thinks workers won't be motivated in cold weather. I really think the motivation is their problem. It appears that if one person vetoes, the answer is no, because it doesn't seem right to strong arm the other one into doing something on their house that they don't want.

According to Dworin in his book <u>Profits in Renovating Older Homes</u>, it is cheaper to hire someone who does the work as a second job. This is probably true, but the other side of the coin is that their main job gets first priority.

Projects Remaining at Year End

1. *Repair living room ceiling; paint living room, hallway and bedroom.*
2. *Install chair railings in kitchen, install new backsplash, obtain pantry closet, buy and install additional cabinets and counter top.*
3. *Obtain new garage door, tarp garage floor, install shelves, organize storage material into plastic boxes, fix foundation crack.*
4. *Assemble computer workstation; unpack computer materials into the shelves and drawers.*

5. Get additional sump pump, lay vapor barrier.

6. Caulk area between garage roof and bedroom slider doors.

7. Build new entryway decks at front and back, new railing for the roof deck.

8. Refurbish pond, remove old pathway lights and install new ones.

9. Pump septic holding tank, adjust system.

10. Wildlife control.

January: HUD research; chair rail; all painted; VA disappointment; ceilings on the wall

1/11

We cut the amounts of chair rail we need, using the store's miter box.

1/12

The chair rail is stained and left in the garage to dry.

1/14

The larger sections of chair rail in the hallway are mounted. I notice that one section of existing door trim is badly cut - not level and a half inch short on one side. I will get some door casing and trim it correctly. I begin to cope the small sections adjoining the chair rail. The painstaking work is to be done little by little. After a good start, I'm ready for the longest wall section for the kitchen. The old trim is removed with a putty knife and a crowbar. A butter knife is the best tool for removing the smallest corner sections without splitting them. The area under the old trim contains a strip of the old photo finish-type paneling. I have to touch this up to match the rest of the new paint. The rail piece is too long to handle easily. Since I'm alone, I use Arnie's suggestion: I put some dabs of rubber cement on the back of the chair rail to hold it in place temporarily while I nail it in. This works. I think glue might be too permanent, in case it has to be removed for the next painting or in the event I don't position it correctly the first time. I'm very pleased with the new, elegant look, but too tired to begin the next piece. Often, if I push myself in situations like this, I make mistakes. Better to wait till tomorrow. I return to coping. As I am doing this I realize that because the complementary shape is being cut, two could have been done at the same time. This piece is too short to do two. Just as good progress is being made, the coping blade breaks. It's too late for the hardware store. It takes 15 minutes to clean up.

1/15

   Martin Luther King, Jr. Day. Vinnie & Marian will come tomorrow,

Thursday, and probably Saturday or Monday to work on the living room ceiling. There are more holes in the soffit to be fixed, too.

1/16

Vinnie and Marian arrive a half-hour early. I'm glad that I slept in my clothes - we wouldn't have been ready if I didn't. Arnie shows Vinnie the holes to be fixed. They are using tall ladders today for the cathedral ceilings. We have heard rustling upstairs. Arnie calls a pest control company that says they get rid of squirrels and other large pests. They advise us simply to close up any holes we find. Then, when the roof is done, any other entries can be identified. This was free advice, very reassuring, for which we are grateful. We will surely hire them in the future.

Vinnie mentions that his friend obtained pressed tin ceiling tiles, and they look very fine. He says his friend paid $6.00 a foot at the home improvement store. We're still tending to do a simpler job, but the old tileboard would still have to be removed, and whatever is under it should be smoothed. One part of this job will require removing the window trim, which is poorly installed. I think that as long as Vinnie has to do that anyway, and cuts needn't be made around the window stool (the trim under the sill), we should reconsider it. At the home improvement store the tiles are $8.49/sq.ft, except for white, which we don't want, which is about $4.00. We don't see exactly what we want, either. I decide to go back to the Internet. I find what I want in Texas for $2.25/sq.ft, $25 packing fee and $45 for express delivery. This makes $3.25/sq.ft. I won't have to wait 7-10 days for delivery, and I won't have to depart from the design I've chosen. Hooray for the Internet.

1/17

When I do my usual search on www.hud.gov I find that the little "artist house" in Rockville is listed again. This time one doesn't have to be an owner-occupant. It appears this is the second fall-through. I find this just as Arnie has said he would take a cheap condo in that area for a pied-à-terre and fix it up himself if it was in a bad neighborhood, so as not to endanger me. I think this is perfect, but since there's now a daily deadline, it might even be gone by tomorrow noon. Arnie calls Joe Thomas, our previous agent, and arranges that we will start driving to Rockville at 11:00 a.m. HUD says they report at noon. We will call Joe at 1:00 p.m. If the house is taken, we will turn back. If not, we will go forward to see it. It would not be prudent to bid on it sight unseen.

At 1:00 p.m. Joe reports it is still available. We arrive at the house at 3:15. The neighbor with the car and other furniture in his front yard has just come home with a 24-pack of beer. He stops to chat with us. He gives us the skinny on the house. It has been empty for 10 years. There are stones in the sewer line, and the raised parking lot of the courthouse behind us spews water that floods the back yard after rain. He himself is on disability, says he fixes antique cars to keep him free of medication, and he isn't going anywhere. The block once harbored drug dealers, but they are now gone. A house here recently sold for $74,000. When I tell him another on this block recently sold for $85,000 he seems shocked.   After a bit more chatting, he goes inside.

We wait in our car for Joe.   When Joe arrives he has bad news.   The house has been sold under the Officer-Next-Door program, a HUD program designed to offer special advantages to police officers who are bidding on HUD houses.   We wouldn't have had a chance. Curious, we go inside nevertheless. The house is very tiny.   The floors are springy.   There are no kitchen fittings to speak of, just a stove of questionable function and a rusty metal cabinet, sink and counter. The floor coverings are shot - thin carpet, black with dirt; parquet-type vinyl tiles, warped and broken. The bathroom can't be tested, as the water is turned off.   In the little back yard some of the neighbor's equipment, ladders and lumber, are overhanging this property.   There is a volunteer willow tree starting to grow there.   Joe tells us a property at the end of the block is for sale for $95,000, but he thinks that's too high.   However, the records of comparable sales he brought show a house in that row sold for $89,000 very recently.   Joe expects to get a digital camera, so he will be able to send us pictures by the computer if a likely house comes onto the market in the future.

While driving home, we do some figuring. We think the cost of repairing such a house would be $17,500. We can't see any way we could reasonably have bid on this house. Its $69,000 price plus $17,500 for repairs takes it to $86,500. That doesn't include our labor, which we now understand is considerable. Additionally, the eccentric next door neighbor makes it a risky business. I had been thinking that at worst it would be a possible short-term furnished rental for the various corporate people and researchers who come to the area, but we see it would not be suitable for this function. Finally, we decide we are happy it was sold, because there would not be any conflict.

1/19

On the Internet, I find a house which is available through the Veterans Administration. It's at the price we want and in the area we want. This gives Arnie a problem, because after our trip to Rockville we had talked about a small apartment in the Capitol district of Washington. We call the VA agent in Silver Springs, leave a message.

The ceiling tiles that I ordered do not arrive. I call Texas and have to leave a message. I guess everyone leaves early on Fridays.

1/20

Vinnie the Plasterer doesn't show up at 9:00 a.m. He calls and pleads snow. (We had two inches of snow, a baby amount in this area.) He will come around noon. He and Marian arrive, work about 15 minutes and then leave.

1/21

I work on the rest of the chair rails. Six inches of snow fell overnight. The morning is spent clearing snow. The VA lady, Phyllis, returns our call, says she can send us a photo of the house via the Internet about seven or eight o'clock tonight. At 10:30 p.m. we have no news. Arnie e-mails her at the address she gave him, giving her a chance to verify that she has our correct e-mail address.

1/22

Early morning, and we have received e-mail from Phyllis, stating the house is still available. We can't retrieve the photo she has sent us, as it is not in a file with a photo suffix. She has seen the house, and it's "not in a bad neighborhood," has a garage that an owner started changing into a sort of workroom, but it was not finished. There were no appliances. She suggests we bid on the house and withdraw our bid if we see it and don't want it.

We drive more than 200 miles to meet Phyllis at the Rockville house at 3:30 p.m. The house has lots of space, with the garage as she described, really a mess, but salvageable; a tiny bedroom adjoining it, different from the rest of the house; a bathroom with a Jacuzzi; another with a shower surround, okay fixtures; hardwood floors in the living room; a master bedroom; a small kitchen with no appliances but a broken dishwasher, good cabinets with one door missing; a laundry room with a new washer, a questionable dryer, a broken water heater; an attic with storage, a stand-up section over the garage, a room begun but not finished; a nice garden; a good deck. We are happy we bid. Phyllis thinks we will get it at our bid price of $1,500 over the asking $106,000, net to the VA a bit more than $100,000. We are happy coming home, but trying hard not to make plans, as we really don't know if we'll get it. The more we think about it, though, the more we like it. We get home after 10:00 p.m., try to get to sleep because Vinnie is coming early tomorrow to finish painting the living room and the stairway area.

We have a message from Texas that the tin man mailed our order for 1/19 delivery, and the delivery company says we weren't home.

1/23

Early morning - we look under "Properties Under Contract" on the Veterans Administration web site and find another bidder has offered $160,000 for this $106,000 house. No, it isn't a number reversal. This is sad. We don't want to hop over to Maryland again so soon. We feel all Rockville'd out. We had best get new plans.

In the meantime, Vinnie, Marian and their son have arrived to paint.

I call Texas to get the tracking number for the delivery company. The automatic tracking record shows delivery first on 1/22, and we weren't home. They will attempt again today. Wait a minute! What happened to the 1/19 delivery? I call for a human. She checks and says there was a delivery 1/19, 6:00 p.m. Both Arnie and I were home, and there was no delivery. Further, no delivery notice was left. I tell her how disappointed I am. Here it is Tuesday the 23rd, and I still don't have my tiles. Chris will call me. He does. I get many different versions of this delivery, such as "first attempt on 1/19," "first attempt on 1/22." I ask how that can be. He replies, "Well, maybe it was the bad weather on the 19th." It's always bad weather in the Poconos. That's why it's a ski area. In fact, there was a threat of a storm forecast for later that night, but that day was fine. Then he tells me it was sent third day air delivery, not two-day air delivery. I tell him I paid for two-day and ask him what the difference is between two- and three-day delivery. "One day." He can't tell me the rate. Marian thinks this is very funny. She guesses he answered, "one day." "Just like a man," she says. I am happy that the shipment is not lost. Chris will tell the deliveryman that we will be home today to receive it.

By the afternoon, the living room and stairway area is all painted. This is a milestone. The entire house is now painted.

In the evening, the tin ceiling panels arrive. Our usual driver was not on duty on the 19th. It seems apparent that his substitute attempted delivery to the wrong house. I really like the panels. I have ordered trim that's a lot wider than I thought, but this is a minor point. I call Vinnie to tell him that the tiles have arrived. I am to call him Wednesday evening for a possible Thursday appointment.

The Living Room Project

1. *Clean cobwebs from walls.*
2. *Wash thick dust off ceiling fan.*
3. *Change ceiling fan light shades to a more sophisticated style.*
4. *Clean windows, install roman shades and curtains.*
5. *Clean carpets - wasted.*

6. Paint edges of walls and stairway where new carpet will be installed.
7. Order carpets (three attempts)and have them installed.
8. Choose and order heating system for the fireplace.
9. Obtain gas service and a gas tank for fireplace, and connection for second heater.
10. Order additional gas tank and have it installed.
11. Remove rust from front door; paint front door; paint exterior of front door.
12. Replace weather-stripping for front door.
13. Remove old torn hardware cloth from window screens and replace with new.
14. Paint one long wall.
15. Find, order, receive delivery and assemble four wall units.
16. Have retaping of failing taped joints in ceiling.
17. Have streaked plaster scraped, new plaster applied to stained areas of ceiling.
18. Obtain desired paint. Have sloping ceiling and three other walls painted.

19. *Repair doorframe with epoxy wood.*
20. *Match paint to wood stain, paint doorframe and sand.*
21. *Prime and repaint stained section that reappeared through the paint.*

1/24

We had a blackout overnight, after an old empty building on the main road burned down. It is estimated we won't have service until 11:00 a.m. The electric heat in the bedrooms has been off since 3:30 a.m. We use the wall gas heater as a backup to the main gas heater, as the main heater depends on an electric fan to distribute the heat. It warms the main areas very well. We close off the electrically heated areas to conserve heat, except for the bathrooms. The electricity comes on well before 11:00 a.m.

1/25

I had washed and ironed all the curtains while the living room was being painted. I rehang them today, clean the windows, and replace plants I had removed to the guestroom to protect them from paint fumes. Arnie rehangs paintings and posters. I go to pick up my new eyeglasses. When I return home, I find the effect of the living room very pleasing.

We have an appointment with Vinnie to install the tin ceiling tiles as kitchen backsplash at 8:30 tomorrow morning.

1/26

Vinnie is able to remove the tile board without pulling down the drywall. The biggest problem will be the outer edges, possibly a corner. After various solutions are considered, Arnie offers the best ones: if we don't use centering under the window, the corners will include whole squares, so the design comes smoothly around the corner; at another tricky edge the circular design helps - a quarter strip completes the circles. Using a four-inch unit design has helped keep the symmetry. A six-inch or one-foot design would have presented harder design problems at the edges. The final product is rather dramatic. Vinnie asks $50 for three hours' cutting edge work. "On-the-job training," he says, but Arnie feels it is really worth much more, so they compromise at $75.

I call Kenny, who did the landscaping, and who will try unusual tasks, to arrange to assemble the computer desk, which has been waiting in the garage, and to arrange for delivery and assembly of a kitchen pantry. He will pick it up at Home Depot, where he has to go anyway. We would just as well pay the delivery charge to him. We will arrange to do it the weekend after Super Bowl Sunday, a sacrosanct weekend in this area. Since we don't know what this job should cost he will do it on his hourly fee of $20/hour, and $35 for delivery of the pantry. He may bring his assistant, Tom.

1/27

Droopy day. I want to sleep late, as we have had two nights of short sleep, one for the fire alarms and consequent blackout, one for meeting Vinnie in the morning. I do just a little bit - measure door trim twice and cut it short once. More trim will be needed. A bit of wall is showing between the new tin tiles and the upper cabinets, because the cabinet is not quite level, which Vinnie pointed out yesterday. Arnie fills it with gray Mortite® caulk, a caulk in rope form, which can be molded to fit. Now, it's perfect. Also, Vinnie righted the window trim and apron, which was installed off level, also. Therefore, I had to use wood putty filler to fill gaps left by the crooked alignment. It fits now, but there is a strip of the old pink paint left showing. I'm beginning to accumulate paint touch-ups and will set aside a day to do them.

1/30

I pay for a pantry at Home Depot and arrange that Kenny will pick it up. I call Kenny to tell him it is done, give him an order number, just in case, and verify our appointment for February 3.

February II: Inside jobs - some assembly required; kitchen cabinets

Kenny the Landscaper and his assistant, Tom, arrive in a flurry of snow plowing. Kenny does snow plowing for his neighbors in a nearby development, and there has been plenty of snow. He takes a few swipes at the snow in our driveway as he arrives. The pantry they are to assemble weighs 125 pounds, but they scoff at the idea of emptying the carton a section at a time. In a couple of hours they have assembled the pantry. They take a cigarette break, then move on to the task of putting together the computer desk. The desk is a lot more complex and takes longer. Through the afternoon I hear their murmuring as they discuss the instructions. I admire their persistence. They take short breaks for smoking, lunch on hero sandwiches they brought with them. They never use the bathroom. They never show signs of short temper or exasperation. By late afternoon I have a computer station. This means

I can completely update all my computer accessories and place them in the desk. At night, Arnie rewires my computer and printer for me. The computer loft project is completed.

Computer Loft Project

1. Paint margins of walls adjoining old carpet, preparing for laying of new carpet.
2. Purchase new carpet, have old carpet removed, and arrange for new carpet installation.
3. Clean high windows, polyurethane sills.
4. Have holes in soffit drywalled.
5. Have walls and stairway painted.
6. Change switch plate.
7. Shop for computer station, find it out of stock, phone order, have it delivered to store, drive 30 miles each way to pick it up and bring it home, unload it into garage.
8. Arrange for assembly of computer station.

2/7

Today is spent doing paint touch-ups. I have streaked the Formica countertops by laying a bottle of harsh chemical on them. I have camouflaged the damage by painting spatters to match the existing pattern. Three coats of polyurethane go over my "*faux* Formica" counters.

Making it Worse

Sometimes you can make things worse. I did. I used an excellent product for cleaning ingrained stains in tile and grout and old porcelain tubs. But then I put the bottle down on the Formica kitchen countertop, with its special sponge, marring the counter permanently. The company's customer service department informed me the main ingredient was phosphoric acid, and nothing could be done to neutralize the "etching." My solution was to match the Formica color and paint it, trying to mimic the spatters with marking pens, a sort of faux Formica, and then to polyurethane it with three coats. It looks neat and workmanlike, but I started with a factory finish.

I fill in the pink area that was revealed after the kitchen window frame was made level and plumb. Areas near the trim and moldings in the guestroom need refining. In the bathroom, a few paper leaves near the radiator came loose from the wall and had to be removed, leaving dried, alligatored glue. I remove the spots with wallpaper remover, which actually loosens glue, and repaint them.

In the hallway, the paneling was asymmetrical on the two sides of the door, a thin strip only drywalled on one side, while the wider side is paneled. I paint that strip the same color as the paneling, to create the impression of symmetry.

I have noticed a scar of the old chandelier on the ceiling and paint it out.

Two stains reappeared on the newly painted wall in the living room. I wanted to use stain killer-type primer on them and then repaint. Arnie thought you wouldn't need stain killer, just repainting would do it. We agreed to do a controlled experiment. I paint my stain with the stain killer-type primer, allow it to dry, then repaint with white latex. When he comes home he gives his stain two coats of latex paint. We will see.

2/17

The stain shows through the paint only area. The area with primer stays white. Now we have information.

I have been working on a piece of door trim that wasn't hung level. The miters don't fit into the vertical angles. One side is just lopped off where it meets a wall. I've realized trim is cheap and not worth skimping on. The trim for this house appears to be standard. Here I've been, sculpting a piece of marred door trim, when it's much easier to remove and replace it. I cut two pieces, then, for both doors. It takes another day to stain them and let them dry. It's now clear they didn't fit because the vertical trim was not plumb. Arnie sands a drop with his Dremel to get a slightly better fit. The rest can be puttied in.

I do a real Laurel and Hardy job of attaching the trim the first time. On one door I've been nailing the trim into a gap, so it isn't holding. The other side isn't holding either. Arnie tries to help me by removing the nail, and the wood cracks. I decide I'll have to do this again, meaning another trip for wood plus recutting and restaining, so I remove the whole thing, cracking the other side in the process. When the piece is down, Arnie sees that I've been trying to nail down over a series of nails that aren't holding anything. "Nail shim," he calls it. He removes the nails, thinks the cracked pieces can be glued, tries it with a super glue, which doesn't hold, then with carpenter's glue, a very nice job. It is set to dry.

2/18

A very small amount of stained wood putty makes the mars on the trim invisible. Finally, I can nail the trim sensibly. I do a neat job of the putty, and the trim looks much better. Of course, since it is now set on the level, a bit of the old pink paint is showing. I don't save this for touch-up day, even though it's inefficient to do it now, because it will complete the hallway.

Tomorrow we plan to start the process of replacing the garage door.

Hallway Project

1. Paint candy pink walls a cream color above wainscoting.
2. Paint wainscoting Federal blue.
3. Have old carpeting removed and replaced with a pale brown one. Replace metal threshold leading to bathroom.
4. Match missing baseboard trim to kitchen trim, which is around the corner. Cut with miter box to fit. Stain. Cope inside corner piece. Nail in.
5. Remove narrow, plain molding above panels. Replace with stained chair rail to run continuously with the kitchen rail.
6. Match two-inch strip adjoining laundry closet with Federal blue paint to mimic paneling on opposite wall.
7. Remove crooked door trim. Cut and stain new piece and re-install.
8. Correct paint over the now level door trim.

Arnie has changed his mind about starting on the garage door, talks about its being too cold for the installers. I ask him why he said yesterday that he would do it. He replies it was warm yesterday. I remind him that they are probably not coming right over. He consents to my making an inquiry. I think it's too cold for him. It is true that he often has to interface with the workers, and we've had plenty of 18-degree days.

2/18

The repaired guestroom door now looks whole and elegant. I hadn't realized what an eyesore the trim was. In fact, all the trim I've done looks better than the original. The original looks flat and has no grain to it. I have stained mine with a standard stain and sanded it, and it looks like it's a better quality, although it's just plain pine. This is not a high priority job, but I will think more about it.

I go to Home Depot to check out garage doors and kitchen cabinets. The waiting list for garage door installation is four weeks. The kitchen cabinet news is not too good. The style I want for a wall cabinet and a base cabinet will be $325 and $450. This doesn't include installation or a countertop. I think $1,000 is out of proportion for this house. A set of cabinets from a popular decorating warehouse would be about $500, but the nearest store is located about 100 miles away. There would be shipping charges. The pieces are knockdown and include separate doors, shelves, hinges, sides and backs. The salesperson was unsure about the components. It seems very risky. If something goes wrong we will have to drive 200 miles to correct it. Then we would first have to obtain a countertop and an installer. Arnie suggests I compromise with a setup by the original installer, very traditional and inexpensive. The extra money can go into something else, such as improving the countertops. This is fine. I go to the manufacturer's site on the Internet and find their dealer just a few miles away. This is not coincidence. For many years this local home improvement and lumber store was the only one for miles around. In another house we had, the medicine chest was broken. It had unusual dimensions, but I found the exact model in this nearby store, probably where it was first purchased.

2/19

I call the hardware dealer to check that they carry this line of cabinets. They do, and the purchase goes smoothly. They have butcher-block countertop in stock, too. The cabinets will be delivered around March 2. Vic is the man to install them. Charles the Cabinet Man thinks Formica countertop might be laid over the old one if the old is in good condition. I call Vic and leave a message.

2/20

Vic can install the cabinets. I'm to call him when the cabinets are actually here. Installation is $150. He says a Formica re-do is not possible; the whole countertop would have to be replaced. We'll keep the *faux* Formica.

I order knobs and pulls now that I know what cabinets I will have. At present, the cabinets have none, which is putting wear on the most-used drawers. The hardware will cost $186 for 24 pieces, which seems exorbitant. But they don't cost much more than the moderate ones, and these will be stylish for a longer time.

2/21-2/28

Outside work can't be done, and inside work is nearly complete. We will wait for the cabinets to arrive.

March II: Kitchen cabinets; garage door opener; garage door

3/3

I call Charles the Cabinet Dealer. He checks on my order, which should have arrived yesterday. He explains that one of the cabinets had been discontinued. Aristokraft was going to make it on special order (I think that is very nice of them), but it should have been in anyway. He will check on Monday.

We stop at Home Depot on our way to the movies and order a garage door. We decide on a middle-priced door, a savings of $220 over the premium door. The premium has similar construction, with a minor design change in the raised panel, a feature we don't think makes a significant difference in its appearance. The dealer will come to measure, then fill our order within three weeks.

I call Charles the Cabinet Dealer to find out about the kitchen cabinets. He is off on Thursdays.

3/11

The kitchen cabinet hardware arrives. I realize I forgot to call about the cabinets.

3/12

Charles the Cabinet Dealer tells me he remembered me but he forgot to call the manufacturer. He'll check his paper work. No, it hasn't arrived. He'll call again Monday. Two hours later he calls again. In fact, the cabinets are there. They'll be delivered in an hour or so. Their driver has to do a bit more shoveling of the driveway to get his hand truck through. He can't get the heaviest cabinet up the stairs, so we leave both in the garage. I figure we can remove the drawers at installation time to get it into the kitchen. I check superficially, just to make sure it's the right color.

I leave a message with Vic the Installer to have the cabinets and counter top installed.

3/17

Arnie wants to work on obtaining a remote to open the garage door, more convenient than negotiating an icy path in bad weather. There appears to be a Sears keypad already on the jamb. He buys a replacement keyboard apparatus. The instructions are missing. He drives back and makes an exchange. When he studies the new directions he finds they are too elaborate, requiring drilling special holes in the jamb, extending wires through the garage, and ladder work at the opener.

3/19

Vic the Installer calls and apologizes for not calling on the weekend. Can come around noon. He finds the base cabinet broken in several places. He says this is common in kitchen cabinet delivery. He thinks it fell off the truck. I call Charles the Cabinet Man. He seems skeptical when I tell him the cabinet is broken in a few places, so I suggest Vic may be able to describe it more accurately.

Vic describes it to him this way: Let's say the box was standing in your side yard, and let's say I was in my truck, going 45 miles an hour, and I hit it. That's what's wrong with it.

I have to provide my receipt number for a reorder. Charles apologizes. Vic and his very pleasant assistant, Chuck, hang the wall cabinet. I ask Vic if he can fix an existing cabinet door that doesn't close completely and doesn't seem to be plumb. When he examines it he thinks the problem is deeper. The floor of the cabinet is sagging, causing a slight separation in the frame. To fix it, he would have to redo some of the undersink plumbing, which he thought should have been done through the crawl space, originally. He tells me the current arrangement might lead to leaks. We understand that there's a difficulty here, but the solution is more costly than the benefits we think we would obtain. We will wait until some other problem arises in this area, and then we will address the door as an add-on.

The wall cabinet is a handy addition to the kitchen. The men take pains to hang it evenly. I offer a check for work done so far, which seems to be appreciated. They load the damaged base cabinet onto their truck to return to the home improvement store. Charles calls again to tell me the base cabinet is in stock and will probably arrive at his place tomorrow.

Later, I realize I should actually have gotten a receipt for the returned cabinet, but since the home improvement store is aware of it, and many of these transactions are really informal contracts, I think we're all right with this.

Arnie comes home with new devices for fixing the garage opener remote system. This universal remote requires wiring to the garage door opener itself rather than the jamb. The garage door has a manual opener inside the garage. If you press a bar the garage door opens. Press again and it closes. Arnie takes the opener apart, removes the wires from inside the circuit box and wires the manual and the remote together. The door opens. He also bought a remote controller for the manual controller, and it now controls the door from outside as well.

Arnie's temporary solution for the sagging cabinet floor is to prop it up from within with wooden shim.

3/20

Charles the Cabinet Dealer is not in today.

3/21

Charles tells me that the supplier came to pick up the old cabinet, but didn't have a new one, so his store didn't release it. Today he phoned and was shunted through various bureaus and changes in the supplier's company. The new cabinet is expected Friday or Tuesday. Therefore, Vic and I have to make a new appointment.

Home Depot phoned to time the new garage doors for Tuesday.

The white kitchen storage cabinet needs some decoration. It is too boxy and too stark white. I have been planning to antique it. I sand it, base coat it with a plum-colored paint and let it dry for 24 hours.

I have bought sets of knobs for the kitchen cabinets and begun marking them for placement. I notice another set of doors out of alignment. Arnie examines them and finds that if he applies shim inside the hinge the doors hang straight. He thinks this might work for the undersink cabinet door, too.

3/22

I apply a coat of crackle glaze over the plum painted cabinet, let it dry an hour, then apply an off-white paint. The glaze cracks the white paint here and there, so that streaks of plum show through, suggesting an old cabinet. Tomorrow, I will dilute some brown furniture stain, saturate a pad of cheesecloth with it and wash it over the whole thing to make it look old. I also have some rope molding to soften the edges and doors, and marble-type knobs. This type of cabinet will add variety and some color to the bank of oak boxes that make up the kitchen cabinetry.

3/23

I work on attaching some pulls, knobs and handles to the kitchen cabinets. The screws provided aren't quite right. They come through to the back of the doors a bit. They are also not quite tight in the pilot holes, but a smaller drill bit is too small. One screw head comes off completely when almost in the hole. Removing it with a wrench would take too long. I hacksaw it off, since it's the first one to be installed, then lower the handle a quarter-inch so that the handle covers the screw. I have no patience left to measure out the location of some of the drawer pulls, so I stop for the day.

3/26

Vic the Installer returns my second call about attaching the base cabinet in the kitchen. We decide to play it by ear. He will call sometime during the week when he can squeeze it in and when the weather is good enough that he can deliver it in his pickup.

3/27

The Home Depot Garage Man arrives at 8:00 a.m. promptly, works till 10:30 a.m. The new garage door looks very neat. I think it makes a big difference in the approach to the house. It looks as though it has always been there. The installer asks me how you find foreclosures. When I mention the Internet, his face falls. He is not a computer man. I tell him about a Realtor who had a FreddieMac and who offers foreclosure lists.

3/28

Vic calls, then comes after lunch. He and his assistant do a fine job with the base cabinet. They, too, find the screws turning round and round in the hole, although the pulls are attached well. He suggests getting a slightly larger diameter screw and putting a nut in the back to shield the point.

April II: Kitchen cabinets done; spring flowers; a new back stairway

4/2

We've been working out schemes to measure kitchen drawers for a cup-type pull. However, the pulls are in a spot where I can't see the level easily. I do it badly, and the screw head breaks off. Arnie gets it out with a wrench, but the new screw head comes off also. He takes the drawer pull with him to the hardware store and gets new, stronger screws. They don't match exactly, but are not noticeably different.

4/3

Now the drawer hardware work goes more easily. The screw fits the drilled pilot hole better, and the cordless screwdriver fits into the head of the screw correctly. I'm not struggling with the level. Finally, all the kitchen cabinets have knobs and pulls.

4/5

The snow is melting at last. We think we can plan new porches and decks to replace the broken and rotting ones. Although we wanted Tommy the Carpenter, Arnie points out that he didn't return our calls on both occasions when we called him last summer. We consider Vic, because he did an excellent job on the cabinets. We decide to call him to do the smaller outside stairway. If he does well on that, we will ask him to make a front entryway. Arnie asks what I think it will cost. I think the back steps will cost about $350, maybe a little more.

4/6

Vic calls. We arrange to speak again after Easter. He thinks $300 to $400 when I ask about a price range, explaining he said $400 so that he shouldn't ask too little and then have to stick with it. He assures me he will not try to soak us. I think it was sensitive of him to sense our reluctance to pay a premium price for a back stairway.

4/13

Finally, a good garden day. I assemble a copper bird bath, fill the stand with rocks for stability, spray hot pepper wax where squirrels have begun to dig for bulbs, plant two *Pieris* and a boxwood, clear a wild section of periwinkle and adjust the grading away from the house with extra soil. Then I replant the pulled periwinkle to grow in a more orderly fashion. I cut sprouts from a stand of stumps, which I plan to mask with some silver fleece vine. I choose that plant because I have seen some growing near the roadsides, so they might be successful here. I assemble a solar path light. The stake provided does not seem to fit into the tube indicated. Arnie cuts one flange from the stake, which works. Then he realizes that bending the flanges will work. The second light assembles in a minute. The fancy address plaque I have stored since December can be staked into the ground. Arnie thinks it looks too industrial. I think it's elegant, and it has cost much more than I wanted to spend. We will see what to do. Perhaps a pot of flowers beneath the plaque will soften it.

We're planning to call Norm the Roofer after Easter.

4/15

Easter Sunday, beautiful and serene. A mail order garden store had reshipped plants that arrived frozen last month. They had stated their ship date was 4/29, but here they are. I plant three foxgloves, soak the three butterfly bush plants in water until tomorrow, continue to cut out sprouts and some thorny devil's walking stick from the stump area. The winter aconite is flourishing, more bulbs are emerging. This is beginning to resemble a garden. So far, woodland creatures have eaten nothing.

4/16

Tonight, we have a light snow and freezing temperatures. I fear for the new plants, but they seem to be all right.

4/17

Vic calls early and speaks to Arnie. He didn't want us to think he forgot about us. He says this twice. There will be rain this weekend, but he will come around and look at the back stairway between appointments and schedule when there's better weather. I think that's awfully nice, and hope that made as good an impression with Arnie, who is still cautious about him.

4/24

Kenny the Landscaper returns my call requesting that he put us on his list for a spring cleanup of the grounds. He can do this on Saturday on his way back from an estimate he is making in a development right behind ours. We will also discuss some tree trimming, and we will plan the pond. I want to show him the wonderful spring garden which has grown in one of the beds he and Tom prepared in the fall. It hasn't reached its peak yet, but is full of narcissi and daffodils, both miniature and full size, aconite and bluebells, puschkinia and squill.

4/27

I missed my appointment with Kenny. I am mortified. Early in the morning, we tried to return a rental car we had while our own was being repaired, but Kenny arrived a few minutes before the stated time, and we missed him. I phone and apologize, but his wife seems to think nothing of it.

Vic was to come, but didn't make it. We'll try for Monday. Arnie and I have another appointment until 2:00 p.m., but Vic is to get started on a back stairway even if we are not there.

4/29

When we return from our appointment, Vic is working on the stairway. After two hours, we have a new back stairway. It is not perfect, but the price was $250, reasonable. It is to be left to dry for two to three weeks, as this lumber has been out all season and is very wet. Then it can be sanded, stained and sealed. It is much sturdier than the old stairway, which had only two posts, one at the head of the stairs and one at the bottom. This one has two balustrades per tread, and they're parallel.

May II: Outside jobs - Spring cleanup; deer-resistant plants; decks and rails

5/3

Kenny the Landscaper will come on Monday. We will walk the whole property and list the landscaping jobs that need to be done.

I put in a call to Vic to install a front deck.

5/6

Kenny calls to change our appointment. One of his workers has "disappeared," and he has fallen behind. He is very apologetic, tells me he hates to do it because we've been customers for years. The category *customer for years* is very interesting. I am very proud to be a customer for years.

I've been working on cleaning the garage in order to clear the kitchen of clutter that is piling up ready to go into the garage, but for which we have no place. We had been to a Poconos Home Show, where Norman's Carpets had a display. Marion the Carpet Lady was there and said she was curious about the house and would like to see it. We invited her to come, so now that someone is going to see it I am more motivated to clear up the clutter.

The front door frame has never been painted and is showing peeling paint. In a few hours the old paint is scraped off, uneven areas are spackled, and it is primed. We want to finish it before the new deck is built. There is some new rust on the front door. Two coats of rust remover are applied. Tomorrow, I'll repaint the entire front door.

It's been a perfect week in the garden. Perfect with regard to the weather - plants are rarely perfect. The bulbs from Dutch Gardens were amazing. There was a good month of flourishing bulbs: daffodils and narcissi, squill, puschkinia, bluebells and snowdrops. Not one was eaten. I saw a few dug up, probably by squirrels, but I replanted them and sprayed with hot pepper wax, which seems to have done the job.

Other plants were a different matter. One company sent me an order in early April, when there was still snow on the ground. The order arrived frozen. Customer service was very nice and said they shouldn't have shipped until April

29.   They re-shipped on April 15.
Nice, healthy plants arrived.   I
planted them, and two days later we
had three days of frost.   Only the
foxgloves survived, but they don't
look green and strong as when they
arrived.   Another nationally known
company shipped at about the same
time.   They sent two small *Pieris*
because the big ones didn't do well
this year, and a boxwood shrub.
They didn't survive the frost,
either.   Only Park Seed sent their
order at the right time.   I started
a patio blueberry and a hardy dwarf
crepe myrtle on the roof deck.

I've also been growing pansies on
a window sill for six weeks.   I plan
to put these in a Posy Pouch®, a
sort of soft hanging strawberry jar.
A plastic pouch is filled with soil.
Slits are cut in the pouch, and
small plants are inserted in the
slits.   The whole thing is hung on a
rail or wall.   I expect to hang them
from a deck railing on the roof.   A
butterfly bush, said to be
impervious to deer, should arrive
soon.   I planted oregano last night.
I will try an herb garden because
deer are said to disdain fragrant
plants.   So far they have not
disturbed lambs' ears (too fuzzy),

Autumn Joy sedum or the foxglove (the source of poisonous digitalis). The barberry bushes, black-eyed Susan, lavender and Russian sage that were planted in the fall have not shown any signs of spring growth. Are they alive? I'll give them two more weeks. I've also been growing some sunflowers sent as a bonus from Burpee, but will wait until almost Memorial Day to put them out in pots on the roof deck.

5/7

The front door gets its final coat of paint. It looks quite tidy and inviting.

5/8

Vic will try to make a Monday time for the new entryway deck. He will bring his assistant, Chuck. They will begin together. Then Vic can drive for any additional materials they might need.

5/9

Kenny the Landscaper and I walk the property. I write down the tasks we want done as we discuss them - trimming low branches, removing fallen logs, blowing leaves away, cutting budding beech sprouts, mowing. Landscaping one-third of an acre will cost $250. He will measure the pond areas for a liner to fit, the most expensive part of making a pond, when he comes to mow. Then he will be able to give me an estimate. He tells me Norm the Roofer is moving back to Queens any day now.

I ask about installing an air conditioner. Arnie has been working on getting an air conditioner upstairs to take the edge off any summer heat throughout the house. Cold air will drift over the railings and into the living room. His plan has evolved through getting an 18,000 BTU air conditioner for the bedroom, which would require installing a 240-volt electrical outlet, to getting two 8,000 BTU conditioners with ordinary electricity, to a 16,000 BTU unit and possibly modifying the outlet to 20 amps. The last will be delivered next week.

I notice slight seam marks along the ceiling. Arnie wants Kevin the Inspector to reinspect some aspects of this house, such as the basement, a crack in the garage foundation and some worrisome lifted shingles that might signal deeper problems.

5/12

Kenny arrives with his assistant, Tom, and his young son, Kenny, Jr. They use heavy machinery to mow grass, whack weeds and blow leaves until the landscape is respectable. Ladders and pruners are used to cut down low and weak branches that are growing close to the house, creating an airier look, especially over the patio. The task takes three men five hours. There are two stumps and three piles of stones and dirt left from some earlier renovation. It would be ideal to level them, but it would be very expensive. Kenny has inquired about a man with a backhoe. His fee is $250 per hour, including travel time to and from a town 25 miles away. Kenny hopes to find someone with a more modest price, as he knows a few people who could use these services and he could contract it out. In the meantime, I will send for a silver fleece vine, a fast-growing vine I have seen around here, and hope it masks the piles of rubble and shoots. Kenny has measured out the ponds. He talks about a lot of money without naming an exact figure. I suggest we do one of the three sections this first year. He will call with a price later in the week.

5/13

A vinyl tile in the kitchen is coming back up. A few attempts to re-glue it have failed. It's just in front of the newly-installed kitchen cabinet and seems a tiny bit large for the space in which it sits. We think the weight of the new cabinet has probably changed the stresses and pushed it forward. I use a T-square to draw a straight line about 1/16" from the edge and remove the excess. The tile now rests concisely in its spot.

We think it will be very costly to replace the roof deck railing, possibly $2,000. It's worth trying to clean and stain it. I will try a small section and see how it looks. Perhaps we can have the shaky parts reinforced. Many of the balustrades are bowed. Two, in a corner, are merely suspended from the handrail and not attached to any crossbar at the bottom.

5/14

Vic and his assistant, Chuck, arrive early to make a front door deck. This is a surprise, as we had agreed he would call if he could make it. I'm in my housecleaning dress, without shoes, and Arnie is hardly dressed at all, but after a quick flurry we can show a presentable face.

We had thought about expanding the entry to include a small porch, but we want to keep the rail for balance in icy weather. Vic suggests a rail on the other side. We also want regular 2x2 balustrades with a horizontal handrail, rather than the slanted balustrades attached to a vertical board construction that is common in this area. He can do this.

The deck Vic and Chuck are building is a pleasant surprise. The planks have been cut on the diagonal, a feature I wanted but didn't dare ask for, with plumb balustrades, neat borders and fashioned handrails. It's a knockout, which I didn't expect after the minimal, functional, back entry. The front entrance is more impressive and welcoming now. We'd better get a fancier mat to harmonize with it.

Arnie asks Vic to look at a crack in the garage foundation. Vic thinks Arnie can either jack up the garage, do the masonry, then let the garage back down, or he could caulk it. Arnie thinks he'll do the last. Vic says it should last for 30 years.

We have been waiting for the air conditioner delivery. They deliver it two hours later than promised, but we're glad it's here. The deliveryman remembers us and that we were fixing the house. He asks if we are still doing work on it.

5/15

We are so pleased with the front deck that Arnie is tempted to replace the roof deck railings entirely. After discussing it, we decide we should not succumb to the treacherous might-as-well's. On some home shows we have seen owners keep upgrading their original plans and order luxuries like gold faucets, granite countertops and whirlpool baths. They seem astonished when their costs run tens of thousands over their original budgets. A little restraint and perspective is in order here, especially as we have just done this with the entry. We at first thought we would just replace the entryway, but when it came down to it we decided on a deck, which raised the cost to $1,100. When Kenny comes to install the air conditioner, we should ask for an estimate on power washing and staining/sealing the railings. I could actually do this myself, but we couldn't haul a rented power washer, and I would have to scrub it by hand, getting up and down ladders to do it. The stain and sealer would similarly have to be done by hand. We are not up to this.

5/17

I wash the windows in the room where the air conditioner is to go. Once it's installed I will never be able to do the job without taking the whole assembly out of the window. To be realistic, this is not going to happen.

5/19

Kenny and his assistant arrive with the truck. Tom loads the trimmed tree limbs left from the spring cleaning into the truck while Kenny and Arnie examine and assess the air conditioner installation. Kenny installs the window brackets. By that time Tom is ready to help haul it upstairs and place it in the window. Arnie had decided not to do a wall installation and disturb the studs. His decision was reinforced when he learned that Sears won't do that type of installation anymore, either.

I plant some miniature roses into containers which will have to go on the roof deck because deer eat roses. It's a perfect planting day. I also put the rest of my seed-grown pansies into a plastic pouch and pot an experimental sunflower, variety unknown, sent as a seed bonus from Burpee. I want to try planting alyssum, as it has an intense, honey-like fragrance said to confuse the deer. Kenny is laughing at me. "Planting flowers for the deer," he says. I have also bought a replacement barberry. Kenny thought the ones I had ordered were dead. The new one seems to like it here right away and is showing off its new pink foliage only two hours after planting.

Kenny and Tom look at the roof deck railing. They think we can shore up the shaky points by installing L-brackets at intervals. Two gallons of stain/sealer should do it. They would have to bring the power washer upstairs, but they think they can do it. It will cost $250. I had actually thought that $200 would be right, but I don't say so. Arnie thinks it's a very fair price because the job will have to be done on two separate days to allow for drying time, and there is the cost of renting the power washer. We set next Saturday, tentatively, as we are depending on the weather to be able to do this job.

5/23

I work all afternoon on the rear patio, hoeing down weeds, emptying bags of pea gravel onto bare spots. Arnie has set up a hammock, some green striped camp chairs, and a bistro set we had from New Jersey.

Now that the weather is warmer, I have set myself the task of working in the garage for 15 minutes each day. Part of the garage is now reasonably organized into like objects together and organized into aisles. I should inform Arnie of my methods. I think he sees the aisles as empty spaces, because he has started filling them in with more stuff. The category "old electronics" seems to be a big one.

We will see if we can designate a particular corner or space for them and then pile them vertically, instead of using floor space for them here and there. That should then free a space that we need for leftover construction materials such as moldings and drywall.

An indoor/outdoor rug for the roof deck arrives by UPS. We won't unroll it until after the railings have been done. It comes wrapped in plastic. We will leave it that way. Rain is expected all weekend, so we don't know when the power washing will take place. Also, Arnie is waiting until there is some dry weather again to call Kevin about a reinspection, as dry ground is better for a septic evaluation. A septic mound should be dusty in dry weather if it is working correctly.

Arnie caulks the cracks in the garage foundation. His neat job makes it look perfectly natural.

5/26

Pouring rain. The roof deck power washing is postponed.

Update: I mention to Arnie that we never followed up on an inquiry about a contractor's discount from Home Depot. Actually, he did inquire. They don't offer material discounts, but will load your truck if you have large quantities. We don't qualify.

June II: Roof deck finished; house presentable; subtotals

6/1

I have asked the carting company to remove garden debris and other trash. Dennis thinks he can come today. I have another appointment from 11:00 to 1:00, but I'm otherwise free. He notes the two hours I won't be here. I am delighted to have such an instant response. Arnie adds some more of his trash and a batch of accumulated cardboard and Styrofoam that is taking garage space. When I return from my appointment at 12:30 I find the trash gone. The truck arrived during my two-hour busy time because they had another nearby pickup. Fortunately, Arnie was here to handle it.

As we are leaving for an evening out, we get a telephone message that unless it's pouring rain, Kenny and Tom will be here in the morning to power wash the roof deck railings.

6/2

I move the plants I have started collecting for the roof garden to a position against the house wall, away from any cleaning compounds that will be used. The men do the power washing in two hours, paying special attention to each rail. Leaning over the rail is hard on the back, so they take turns at it. The railings are unexpectedly transformed from dilapidated to graceful. Kenny and Tom also power wash the siding on the deck side of the house as an extra little fillip to their job. The railing needs to dry today. They will return to stain and seal when two days without rain can be expected. The forecast doesn't make it likely that this job will be finished by June 10, when we have invited a large number of Lapidus descendants to visit for the first time since we moved here. At this point, the roof deck is presentable and glows with potential.

6/9

Kenny and Tom arrive at 8:30 a.m. I am dressed, but Arnie is in deshabille in the kitchen, making a huge potato salad for tomorrow's guests. Kenny thinks maybe he should have called first, but of course we are delighted to see them. We've had rain all week and not much of a chance of nice weather to finish the roof deck by tomorrow. Tom puts a ladder against the side of the house and climbs over the railing onto the deck. The ladder is shaky, and Tom is no lightweight. I am dismayed and point out that he could just as well have come in the front door and used the stairs to the deck. They laugh.

They stain and seal (a product all in the same can) till 12:30 p.m. It looks even better than we thought it would, and we are very satisfied. It was really nice of them to try to make our festivities deadline.

6/10

Arnie's family arrives bit by bit from Philadelphia and Connecticut. One cousin even arrives from a trip he was taking to climb a mountain in Lake Placid. The children are adorable, tumbling in the hammock and playing hide-and-seek among the trees. There's a lot of food and conversation, the house is admired and it is altogether a lovely day.

6/18

The same vinyl tile square in the kitchen has expanded and lifted up. Arnie trims it and fills in tiny gaps with a Mortite® caulk, which matches the edging very well. It is the second time he has done this. He thinks it may need still another try.

6/22

Here are our total expenses so far for repair and refurbishing from 10/15 - 6/21:

Cabinets, shelves and brackets	$ 381.11
Decks & Railings	1650.00
Decorative Hardware	353.85
Drywall and painting	1250.00
Garage Door and Installation	621.11
Heating and cooling items	684.00
Kitchen cabinets and backsplash installation	1063.90
Landscaping	661.45
Paint and supplies	106.27
Plumbing	79.00
Tools and accessories	124.02
Trim	25.00
Miscellaneous hardware	321.76
Illegible item	49.00
Total 10/15-6/21	7370.47
Total from 2/9-10/14	11896.00
Total 2/9 - 10/14	$19266.47

We are not far from our original rough estimate of $20,000 for repairs. Some septic adjustments and possibly basement and roof repairs are yet to be done. We haven't really skimped on much. We just tried to maintain perspective all along, not getting carried away with sub-zero refrigerators or granite countertops, top-of-the-line items that would have been out of proportion for the modest scale of this house. We did spring for good decorative hardware like cabinet knobs and coat racks because they are the costume jewelry of the makeover.

July II: Kitchen project finished, roof maven, septic finished, pond abandoned, basement work.

7/6

I have put off replacing some kitchen molding because it isn't really necessary to the function of the house and therefore gets a lower priority. Now I see that it is the last touch to finishing the kitchen, which would be very satisfying. I decide to overcome all obstacles such as changing my clothes, moving the refrigerator, changing the drill bit, getting out old paint, changing the switch plate, mopping the floor behind the fridge, getting an extension cord so the fridge remains connected, and all those small things that have nothing to do with the actual installation of a chair rail molding.

Installing molding seems so easy, now that I'm an old hand at it. The piece is stained, a backsaw and miter box are used to cut the piece to size, studs are located, and pilot holes are drilled through the chair rail into the studs. Then brads are hammered into the predrilled holes. I'm very proud of my handiwork. The more substantial molding all around the kitchen contributes elegance to the room. The kitchen project is now complete.

Kitchen Project

1. *Have electricity connected from circuit box to proper outlets throughout the room.*
2. *Have undersink pipes replaced and new faucet installed.*
3. *Purchase refrigerator. Have icemaker installed.*
4. *Add an instant hot water faucet.*
5. *Purchase range and dishwasher.*
6. *Clean tops of kitchen cabinets, inside and outside of cabinets, line shelves.*
7. *Purchase two kitchen light fixtures.*
8. *Have electrician to install light fixtures, fix electric range outlet, and attach instant hot water connections, dishwasher connections, and hot water heater.*
9. *Paint bubble gum pink walls cream; paint photo-wood paneling blue; paste wallpaper border near ceiling.*

10. *Buy vinyl tiles for floors and install them.*
11. *Purchase tin ceiling panels and have them installed as a backsplash.*
12. *Repair marred countertops.*
13. *Locate matching base and wall cabinets and purchase them; have them installed with butcher-block countertop.*
14. *Purchase and install knobs and pulls for cabinets.*
15. *Remove minimal moldings and replace with chair rail.*
16. *Replace worn and mismatched outlet plates.*
17. *Purchase pantry; have it assembled; refinish with antique finish. Replace industrial knob.*
18. *Purchase microwave.*

7/7

To remove a red candle wax stain from the stone fireplace hearth we have tried numerous methods and substances: chlorine bleach, a mild phosphoric acid product, antique furniture restorer, paint thinner, paint stripper, heat, ice and a poultice of flour and hydrogen peroxide. None helped. Arnie tries a Dremel, suggests we sand the whole

surface with emery cloth. The
surface grows more whitened and
smooth, with only a faintly darker
mark where the red blotch used to
be. The whole effect is that it
looks nearly new.

7/9

Arnie arranges with Kevin the Home
Inspector to get some advice on the
basement and roof.

I call Kenny the Landscaper, who
says he will get a price for the
pond liner by next Friday.

7/13

Kevin the Home Inspector arrives
with a trainee, Ted. I go to the
library so as not to influence any
discussion of the roof. When I
return, Arnie tells me Kevin's
opinion is that some repairs are
needed: ice guards, definitely; a
kind of renailing in which the nail
is applied and then removed, with
the resulting hole caulked; and
vents. The roof should last 10 more
years. The septic needs a section
of PVC replaced by a plumber. The
holding tank can be pumped, after
which Kevin could certify it. The
basement needs more work. A second
sump pump would help. The leaders

should take water even farther from the house. The main beam is showing a quarter inch of rot. Sistering would help. The beam would last a long time but eventually would fail if left alone. It would help to regrade the land near the house so that water flowed away from the foundation. We will wait for Kevin's written report before deciding how much of these suggestions we will do.

7/15

We have not heard from Kenny about the pond plans. On the Internet, we find a wide price range for pond kits, from $125 to $1,210 for the same size liner. Similarly, a nationally known water garden company charges $49 for a water lily, while a smaller company and Home Depot charge $3. Kenny has said several times that he'll come up with an estimate for the pond, but he seems to forget. I think this is his way of communicating that he doesn't want to do the job. I can't give the job away, though, because that would be disloyal. We consider having the dry pond areas filled in with gravel. We think $1,000 for a pond project is out of proportion for this house, and we worry that children passing by will find the water interesting and might get hurt. We will think about the pond some more.

7/16

We decide to do the noninvasive basement methods and then see if we need to go on to sistering with a pressure treated main beam. If we can dry it out, Tommy's advice that it would right itself if dry may work. So far we have not been able to dry out the basement completely, and so have never followed up on the plan to put Drylok waterproofing on the walls and a vapor barrier on the ground.

7/17

Arnie calls Buck the Septic Man, recommended by Kevin. We would like to get into Kevin's system of contractors. Buck will come on Friday to assess the job. The issue is where the pumping access is located. If at the surface, the tank can be pumped out directly; if deep in the ground, heavy machinery will be needed to get to it.

Arnie installs two more shelves in the garage.

7/18

We really need more shelf space in the laundry room. Every time we do laundry we juggle two baskets of linens sitting on the washer and dryer. Today, Arnie thinks this is not a good system. When he asks me where I want to put the baskets, I am at a loss to think where else they could possibly go. He kindly puts up a temporary shelf until we can design a better system. The washer/dryer hookup and the septic tank alert box are barriers.

7/19

The idea of inserting new vanes in the vertical blind did not work out. The new vanes look nice, but the machinery does not work. We have obtained two new heads with valances. We can use the vanes we recently bought. Arnie installs the bedroom slider blinds, making them level, an improvement over the old blinds. It's now much easier to slide the blinds aside to go onto the roof garden.

Next, he cuts a rectangle of aluminum screening and places it to cover a rectangle of siding which, for unknown reasons, is missing from a soffit.

7/20

Buck the Septic Man is here. He digs out a section of earth near the pumping access. He has good news - the access is only about six inches below ground level. We can pump out the holding tank today without calling for more heavy machinery. The charge is less than half what the national chain charges for pumping out a holding tank. However, the national chain was excellent to use because they responded quickly to an emergency call when we were unable to find anyone else. Buck checks the suspect pipe in the mound and finds it's doing fine, no repair needed. The total cost for all septic repairs was $655. We will now ask Kevin to certify the system, as it is in good shape.

The next step is to get a dehumidifier for the basement and place it so that it empties into the sump pump.

7/21

Arnie installs the new header for the living room vertical blinds.

They go readily into the old brackets. He removes the vanes from the old header and snaps them into the new one. They are still unwieldy. Arnie realizes that although 10 inches were cut from the header, we still have 24 vanes. Removing one vane with its clip from each end solves the problem.

7/25

Arnie buys a dehumidifier, but it's too heavy to move down into the awkward crawl space by himself. I am no help. We will wait until the appropriate person is here for another job.

7/28

Kevin will come on Tuesday to certify the septic tank. He will bring another copy of his report, which he mailed but which we have not yet received.

7/31

Kevin checks the work done and certifies the septic tank, resolving an issue that was unclear since the purchase. He brings his typed roof and basement report. Only minor work is needed on the roof - ice guards and vents, a few lifted shingles, some poorly nailed shingles, but doesn't need reshingling for some years, at which time a better quality shingle should be purchased. As I said, I am delighted to have been wrong and tell Arnie so.

The basement still needs work. Arnie has bought a dehumidifier and will have a second sump dug. Regrading near the foundation can be done manually.

August II: Crawl space plans

8/1

Pete the Plumber will come next Wednesday to install a sump pump and place the dehumidifier so that it empties into the sump.

8/2

We engage Sean the Landscaper to mow the lawn for the rest of the season. Kenny lives too far away to make this job worth his while. Arnie is also thinking Sean might be able to do the regrading near the foundation.

We ask a local Realtor for a referral to a crawl space repair company. He recommends a person who worked on his house and did a good job. This person also does work for his company, a long-established real estate firm in this area.

8/7

Kenny calls. He thinks it's too late in the season to start on the proposed pond and suggests we get someone else. Arnie and I have decided an alternative is to fill it in with gravel rather than soil, because the trenches seem to function as an outside sump. Kenny would still be interested to do it if we decide to go ahead in the spring, but he's just been too busy this year. We are almost sure we will abandon the plans for a pond.

8/8

Pete the Plumber arrives with Charlie, his new assistant. An additional and independent sump pump, which empties into the first sump, is installed on the other side of the basement. It should work well with the newly certified septic system. If it should overload the septic system we will run it into the yard, but it is neater this way because we don't have to make any holes in the building. We also installed the dehumidifier near the sump pump. The water from the dehumidifier drops onto the stones and will seep into the sump. This size dehumidifier is just enough for the entire basement. We should now keep the vents closed so that we don't dehumidify all of the Poconos. It cost $275 for the dehumidifier and $400 for the new sump and pump.

8/15

We receive Kevin's report on the septic tank. It doesn't seem to be an actual certification, just a report on the dye test and on the pipes and alarm system. Did he take "certification" more colloquially than we intended? Arnie calls Kevin about the septic report, which seems a good report, but does not show any official certification. Kevin says he will send us a copy with a certification number.

Arnie goes into the crawl space to close a vent, which has come undone. Now that the new system has been working, a wall which had been glistening with moisture shows some dry spots.

The garage roof shows some condensation.

8/26

Arnie returns to the crawl space. Although some spots are better, others seem worse. Arnie will call Rich the Crawl Space Man. We think this may run into money.

8/27

We have an appointment with the crawl space repairman for tomorrow afternoon, when he will be working in the neighborhood.

8/28

Rich arrives early, very apologetic, but he has just finished working down the street. That's fine with us. He and Arnie go down to the crawl space. Some joists are as soft as butter. The dehumidifier is doing a good job. The sumps need to be dug even deeper, below a vapor barrier which we didn't know existed. The wet wall is composed of concrete block, which may need some grout reinforcement in each block. Insulation board against that wall would save heating costs. Rich will send specific estimates by e-mail and also by regular mail. It sounds like a few hundred here and there, perhaps leading up to a couple of thousand dollars, some of which can be done in stages. It's not as bad as we thought.

8/29

We receive a formal estimate from Rich via e-mail. He divides the job into two parts: crawl space repairs and insulation. We decide he will do the crawl space repairs, but that we can postpone the insulation aspect until next year.   Arnie sets up an appointment for the crawl space repairs for 9/13.

September II: Crawl space repairs

9/1

Kevin comes to the door with a copy of his official-looking certification of the septic system. It's probably more convenient for him to drop things off as he is passing our house than to make a special trip to the post office. The new certification is an actual certificate with an inspection number. All details of the septic inspection are now complete.

9/13

Rich's crawl space crew of three men arrives at 8:00 a.m. They spread black plastic over our carpets on their path to the crawl space and begin work. Rich arrives about an hour later. Beams are sawn which will be attached onto old defective beams, a strengthening process called *sistering.* The beams are passed through outside vents into the crawl space. We can't see how they are being attached, but there is much grunting and calling out. The men borrow some of our simpler tools, such as saws and hammers, because their equipment is actually spread over a few jobs today. A deeper sump is installed, with an appropriate pump. The foundation wall is drilled with weep holes, so that water doesn't lie against it but comes into the crawl space, where it drips out onto the ground. A layer of heavy plastic is spread on the crawl space floor to act as a vapor barrier.

9/20

Kevin arrives in a pouring rain to do a re-inspection of the newly fixed crawl space. He thinks the weep holes in the foundation walls are a good idea. The joists should really be screwed in from the floor above, but since there is an established room with installed carpet, that wouldn't be a practical approach. They might have glued the beams in. The main beam has not been touched. A perfect job would require sistering of the main beam. The plastic vapor barrier is good, and the new deeper sump basket is better. If Kevin were inspecting this crawl space he would not find any major fault with it, but would suggest main beam sistering, an improvement that could cost $1,000 or $300, depending on the contractor. Arnie is thinking of calling Kevin next year to see how the new system is holding up.

9/22

Arnie asks another worker for a price on installing a main beam. His price would be around $300, but he wouldn't be sure until after the job was done.

October II: Fireplace maintenance, market analysis, timber!, punch list

10/1

   The fireplace company is scheduled to come and clean the fireplace for the season and, we think, to identify a slight gas smell Arnie detects. The Fireplace Man thinks that nothing on the roof near the flue would affect the heating unit. He does think that sometimes cleaning compounds or paint combine with the fuel to give a fuel-type odor, or that there would be an odor a while after it was shut off for the season. We agree to a cleaning to see if that does the trick. All seems to be well. The fee is $75. We can call if we detect any odors in the future.

10/3

   Arnie stops in at a large national real estate chain to request an appraisal. The agent at the desk declines to do one, even if it is paid for, unless the house is to be sold. He is helpful, however, and looks in his listing book to find the price of a house for sale just

up our street. The asking price is
$79,000. He suggests that the
Loretta Lewis Agency might do a
market analysis. She says she will
do one for $100, provided it is not
to be used for financial reasons.
We make a Friday appointment.

Loretta the Broker says the house
is adorable. This does not prevent
her from taking extensive
measurements and asking questions
about the basement. She remembers
the house and guesses correctly that
we bought it at foreclosure. She
thinks it now has a homey
atmosphere. Her report will include
sold comparable houses as well as
houses currently for sale. She
expects to be ready by Monday.

10/8

Loretta submits her completed
market analysis. Although it
doesn't include houses currently for
sale, it does include three houses
that have sold this year. One,
which is in this development and
which we have often noticed looks
very much like ours, has sold in
January. The analysis gains
credibility for counting this house.
Two other houses are in the
comparison. Loretta has given us

points for newness: that is, the remodeled features such as new appliances and carpet make it more like a five-year-old house than the 11-year-old structure it is. We get full credit for the cost of the gas fireplace. The other houses are assumed to have been in average condition, but we get an extra $1,000 for good condition. The final estimated appraisal is $74,000. The purchase price was $40,000, with $24,000 going into improvements and repairs. Our gross profit, then, is $10,000, without deducting the closing costs at the purchase or commissions and taxes if we sell it. The results are sobering.

Thoughts about the Market Analysis

The market analysis submitted by the agency seems to be objective. Our house was compared with three other houses in the same or similar developments and which had sold in the past 10 months. One of the comparable houses was almost the same architecturally as ours. The houses were compared feature by feature, with costs added for features our house had that the others lacked, and costs deducted for features the other houses had which our house did not have. Then the amounts were added and subtracted from the actual selling prices to obtain the approximate market value of our house.

Subjectively, one might get more by having attractive landscaping, not included in the comparison. We have a gravel patio area with hammock, table, chairs and umbrella, which we find very useful for entertaining, but it was not computed because it isn't on a concrete slab, and so doesn't qualify as a patio. Likewise, a roof deck with a garden just off the master bedroom is not included in the market analysis, but is a delight. If these features were lacking, we might offer the house for $82,000 and expect to get the $74,000 determined in the appraisal, but given these extras we might get a price closer to $82,000.

10/9

Arnie calls Jake Peterson to look at some trees which could pose a danger this winter. He can trim down the tree whose top fell during an ice storm this winter, as well as prune two others nearby. He expects to do it late this afternoon. He doesn't.

Sean comes with topsoil, grades the wettest side of the house, covers the grading with bark chips and edges the section with stones.

10/10

Jake says he will prune the trees in the next couple of days.

We would like to have thermostats which are more accurate than the ones we have, which are off by 5-8 degrees. Sears thermostats for baseboard heaters are the same as the ones we have. Home Depot can't do better, either. We'll have to make our manual adjustments.

10/11

Jake is here to work on the trees. Arnie takes some interesting photos of him up in the trees with their red fall leaves. Jake does a neat job. The trees look natural, but more important, they will be safe. He shows us another tree in the driveway that should be taken down and that the dead branches of the chokecherry should also be trimmed so that they don't fall on anybody.

We will take care of them in the near future.

> *Punch List - Odds and Ends that remain to be done after the main job is completed.*
>
> 1. Pond excavations to be filled in with gravel, and a stone pond designed.
> 2. Ice guards for roof.
> 3. Extra electric baseboard for the kitchen.
> 4. Questionable tree removed from driveway and split choke cherry branches pruned.
> 5. Insulated board added to one basement wall.
> 6. Main beam in basement sistered.
> 7. Roof deck developed with additional plants and lounge furniture.
> 8. Doors, trim and windowsills sanded and restained.

Assessment

In determining if this project was worth the effort, we considered different aspects of its value.

The Move - In this case we moved into the house we planned to work on, and we are now working on a new house nearby. Are we satisfied to have moved from a New York City suburban area to a semi-rural small town? Yes. We are surrounded by natural beauty, which genuinely touches us. Arnie has always wanted to spend a year in the country, and he has been happy doing so. We have found the country people to be welcoming, more forthright than our suburban neighbors had been, and even eager to be helpful. The only disadvantage to living here has been the lack of available advanced medical care, for which we must travel to the city. A minor annoyance has been the rural mail system, which requires us to get the mail ourselves.

The Purchase - The purchase of the HUD house was very difficult. It took some time to find a Realtor in this area who was computer savvy. We then entered a tangle of bureaucracy and required an attorney's help to get through it. The price of the HUD house seemed fair to us, which may have been the other side of the coin to the bureaucracy: it was originally appraised at $44,000, but never found its way onto the multiple listing, so there were never any bids on it. Seeing no buyers at $44,000, HUD reduced the price to $40,800, and we got it for $40,000.

At first glance, it might seem that an ordinary bank foreclosure would have been easier, but we weren't able to buy one. The bank had plenty of time to wait for the asking price, which was based on the amount of debt rather than the value of the house. Additionally, we did not know that our Realtor for the bank sale was in fact planning to leave her broker and therefore made little effort to close our deal. Negotiations collapsed.

<u>Financial gain</u> - The actual cash layouts were $15,000 for the down payment and approximately $24,568 for repairs and expenses. The monthly mortgage payments

(principal, interest, taxes and insurance) came to $375 per month. If the $15,000 were available in cash we could count on about 6% interest, or $900. Similarly, if we hadn't spent our $24,568 cash for repairs, we could count on over $1,000 interest, but because we actually spent it little by little, you could say we had it an average of half the year, for an opportunity loss of around $660 interest.

We lived in the house, which would command a minimum of $850 per month rent, but we only paid $375 a month to the bank, for a total of $5,700 in rent benefit.

Amount Spent on Repairs

Additional inspections	150
Appliances	$2,964
Cabinets, shelves, brackets	381
Carpet	2,904
Crawl space repair	2,040
Decks & railings	1,650
Decorative hardware	353
Drywall & painting, living room, bedroom, hall	1,200
Electrical	1,276
Fireplace	2,280

Garage door & installation	621
Heating & cooling	1,284
Illegible	49
Kitchen cabinets, backsplash, installation	1,063
Landscaping, miscellaneous, such as hardware, screws, tips, wardrobe	911
Miscellaneous paints & supplies	106
Painting & floor tiles, kitchen	300
Plumbing	1,337
Septic inspection & pumping	225
Tools & accessories	124
Tree removal	245
Trim	25
Window treatments	180
Total	$21,668

Summary

$41,000	Purchase price and closing costs
21,668	Repairs and upgrades
900	Foregone interest on
$15,000	down payment
660	Foregone interest on repair money
$64,228	
-5,700	Rent benefit
$58,528	Total cost
$74,000	Estimated market value of house
$15,472	Total gained

Other gains - We have not included any costs for our physical labor or for the many hours of planning, organizing, directing and coordinating that went into the remodel. The gains from such activities are not apparently monetary, although the knowledge obtained may turn out to be exponentially valuable in future projects. One reward is that the house is exactly to our liking. We were able to pick any paint or carpet color that was available, instead of being stuck with what was in the house or with a contractor's small array of choices.

We took a certain amount of pleasure in solving the problems, knowing that a current headache could be turned into a big benefit. Closing day was a triumph, in view of the pain of the transaction.

We are an even better team for having done this project, each having revealed strengths previously unknown to the other.

We have a wide base of resource people for future projects and for maintenance.

We have a widening supply of tools.

We hope to have helped inform:

- **Readers** by showing a true picture of what it might take to rehabilitate a dilapidated house - what some typical costs are, a few methods of obtaining contractors, how to deal or not to deal with difficult workers, how the weather affects work schedules, to what extent daily life is changed, how to deal with emergencies, and more.
- **Families** who have received an inheritance about a method of investing only some of it for a

down payment on a house while keeping some of it for improvements. In that way they can get a better house and continue to make mortgage payments that are in keeping with their usual income.

- **Workers** who obtain jobs such as defense work, political work or fad industry jobs which will pay well only for a while, that they can buy fixer-upper housing in upscale areas and continue to live in such upscale areas even after the inflated phase of their work has passed.

- **Young people** that they can start in a modest house and use their increasing wages to improve that house as time goes on.

- **Retirees** that they might turn the cash from a lump sum disbursement or the sale of their city or suburban homes into a down payment and repairs. Then they would enjoy reduced payments and taxes while they are on a fixed income. Contact with contractors is a smooth introduction into the community and continued connection with younger people.

- **Creative types** that they don't need to settle for cookie cutter houses or spend everything on their dream home in good condition. They can buy a wreck and shape it to their own vision.

Things that Might have Gone Wrong, but Didn't

1. *There were no requests or hints to make payoffs to officials.*
2. *There were no zoning entanglements involving our proposed improvements - when we needed to remove some trees, the Environmental sub-committee on environment of the development approved within 20 hours.*
3. *Septic repairs were at the low end rather than at the high end.*
4. *We now have a top quality basement for about $2,000. Structural changes and heavy machinery might have been required, but it never came to that.*
5. *The insulation might have been a major problem, but the vinyl siding itself produced a barrier against the wind. Our heating bills were not especially high for this area.*

6. *There were many cobwebs and dead insects when we got the house, but there was no need for extermination, except for the use of Spider-Not®, an environmentally friendly spray. Similarly, wildlife problems faded away once we closed inside holes.*

7. *Largely, all our contractors performed according to our understandings. The one contractor who left the area did not leave with any of our money, and one contractor never began the job, but all transactions were civil.*

Natural Motivation

A feature of this type of real estate project is that the vast preponderance of sub-goals produced are quite naturally definite in concept. These goals tend to be very realistic, tractable, having immediate payoffs upon completion. For example, the goal of plastering the holes in the wall suggests itself each time the wall is seen. A clear vision of its accomplishment also appears. It needs to be done quickly. Nobody will question whether it was worth doing. The skills required to accomplish the task are evident. Ordinarily, the worker gives a clear finishing date. The cost in dollars is clearly measurable. When the task is completed, each time the wall is seen the payoff is evident.

Waiting

In this project, much time was spent waiting - half days for deliveries by merchants, whole days for deliveries from wholesalers to merchants, for people to return from vacation, for people to recover from real or fictional illnesses, for contractors to finish previous job commitments, and hours more waiting for telephone responses to messages left. Most of the waiting was really unavoidable. Arnie tends to be overly patient, so that when the contractor was trying to back out of a simple roof job, he was unaware of it. Nevertheless, there is a lot of waiting, some which can overlap other work.

Community

Changing a substandard, neglected building into a standard, well cared for family house influences the immediate neighbors and the entire neighborhood.

Nobody wants to have the worst lawn in the area. A neglected lawn, such as the one we received from HUD, guaranteed others in the area that their lawn was not the worst. When we cleaned up our lawn, others in the area paid more attention to theirs. We have often refused to consider a house because neighboring houses and grounds were poorly cared for. We're sure Realtors lower expectations for a house near an eyesore. By raising the value of our own property we made the whole area more desirable and valuable.

Informal Contracts

Most of the agreements we had with craftsmen and workers were informal contracts. The common wisdom is to obtain three bids and take the middle one, then check on previous work done in the neighborhood by this person. The work done on our house was most often low priced work. We thought it would be an unfair waste of a contractor's time to obtain bids. If the price seemed reasonable to us, we consented. If it seemed extravagant, we declined it and looked for someone else. If there were several tasks to be done, we might write them down so that nobody would forget the scope of the job. Nobody asked us for a deposit. We would purchase paint ourselves, more because we could get the brands and colors that we wanted than to check on the painters.

Similarly, the contractors didn't check our credit in a formal way that we ever knew about. We paid them by check or cash as soon as the job was finished.

The only job where we received a formal estimate with a cost breakdown of each aspect was for a $2,040 repair of our crawl space. It seemed appropriate to do it that way in this case.

A house maven Arnie knew thought that a homeowner shouldn't worry too much about being cheated on price - the important thing was that the contractor should be knowledgeable and competent. Cheating may not be the issue. For example, sometimes the person can be charging for knowledge. The job will take 15 minutes because she's been doing it for 25 years. The job looks easy, but the person wants to be paid for knowledge, which the average consumer can't evaluate, so she works for seven minutes, goes off to do another job, perhaps, and draws out the job for two weeks, but she isn't really cheating. On the other hand, a high quote or requiring deep excavations without even seeing the job is suspect to us, and sometimes the contractor has in mind a much more elaborate job than we want to do, so we will seek someone else.

The Future

Are there future opportunities for projects such as the one depicted in HUD House?

From the point of view of HUD House, our most recent project is the future. While we were putting the final touches on the house and reworking this book, we started looking for another project. Our plan was to find a government repossession-type house that was bigger, better and in a more prestigious location than the one we worked on in HUD House. We toured at least four repo homes within easy driving distance. We selected one for $80,000. We think that when we are finished we will have spent about $18,000 in repairs and renovations. We wish we might sell it for $135,000, but we'll be happy to make any fair profit.

There are undoubtedly suitable projects to be found on the Internet. As a test, we'll look for something in Las Vegas. Arnie goes to www.hud.gov, and makes his way to the South Central Nevada page via a "homes for sale" link. There are many apparent prospects. One we find interesting is a manufactured home worth $64,000, with two bedrooms, 1.75 baths, with a HUD asking price of $51,202. It should be easier to judge the value of manufactured housing, because it is standard. A good selling point after fix-up would be that when it was in bad condition it was evaluated at $64,000 by HUD. In any case, we guess that the future has easy opportunities for those with energy, optimism and perseverance.

Nancy Lapidus and Arnold Lapidus

Bibliography

Dworin, Lawrence, <u>Profits in Buying & Renovating Homes.</u> Craftsman Book Company, 1996

Irwin, Robert, <u>Find It, Buy It, Fix It</u>. Real Estate Education Company, a division of Dearborn Financial Publishing, Inc., 1996

Mailer, Norman, <u>Harlot's Ghost.</u> Random House, 1991

Means, R.S., <u>Repair & Remodeling Cost Data</u>, R.S. Means Co., Inc. 1999

Reader's Digest <u>New Complete Do-It-Yourself Manual</u>, The Reader's Digest Association, Inc., 1991

Nancy Lapidus and Arnold Lapidus

Index

About the Authors

Nancy Lapidus is a retired high school biology teacher. She is a past president of the New York Biology Teachers' Association, and a founder of the newspaper *Adaptation*, its official publication. She won the Alice B. Crow Award for dedication in counseling with her thesis recounting the mammoth efforts required to originate a drivers' education course in New York City high schools.

Arnold Lapidus started his working life in a gas station when he was thirteen years old. There he picked up knowledge of simple objects like screwdrivers, pliers and Philips head screws. Later he learned about math and computers and used this knowledge in a successful career whose theme has been to make difficult subjects easy to understand.

Nancy has previously bought a fixer-upper for $44,000 and sold it for $73,000. Arnold notes the gross profit is greater than 50%.

Arnie and Nancy currently live in the HUD house in the Poconos, Pennsylvania.

www.ingramcontent.com/pod-product-compliance
Lightning Source LLC
Chambersburg PA
CBHW030255290526
45785CB00001B/96